Business Plan Guide

Simple Steps to Building Business Plans

Steve Maltzman and Mike Benshoof

A Service of

BuilderBooks™
National Association of Home Builders
1201 15th Street, NW
Washington, DC 20005-2800
(800) 223-2665
www.builderbooks.com

Business Plan Guide
By Steve Maltzman and Mike Benshoof

ISBN 0-86718-576-7

Cover design by E Design Communications
Printed in the United States of America

Cataloging-in-Publication Data

Maltzman, Steve.
Business plan guide : simple steps to building business plans / by Steve Maltzman and Mike Benshoof ; National Association of Home Builders, Business Management Committee.
p. cm. – (Pro builder)
ISBN 0-86718-576-7
1. Business planning. 2. Construction industry–Management. I. Benshoof, Mike, 1971– II. National Association of Home Builders (U.S.). Business Management Committee. III. Title. IV. Series.

HD30.28.M3355 2002
690'.8'0684–dc 21

2002154931

For further information, please contact:
BuilderBooks™
National Association of Home Builders
1201 15th Street, NW
Washington, DC 20005-2800
(800) 223-2665
Check us out online at: www.builderbooks.com

01/03 SLR Production/ Data Reproductions Corp., 2500

About the Authors

Steve Maltzman

Steve Maltzman is president of Steve Maltzman & Associates, one of the leading providers of financial and business management services for builders and remodelers. The Redlands, Calif., firm also provides the annual accounting and financial analyses for the 600-plus members of NAHB's Builder and Remodelor 20 Clubs.

Steve is a CPA with over 17 years of experience in the construction industry. He has served as both controller and chief financial officer for various building and remodeling companies. In addition, he spent more than three years as product manager for a leading developer of software for the construction industry and five years as an auditor and consultant for a major CPA firm.

Steve is Past Chairman of NAHB's Business Management & Information Technology Committee and is a member of NAHB's Education & Information Systems Committees.

He is the author of the 1990, 1993, and 1996 editions of the *Remodeler's Cost of Doing Business Study* for NAHB's Remodelors Council and is co-author of the 1990, 1994, 1997, and 2001 editions of the *Cost of Doing Business Study* for NAHB's Business Management Department. He also writes a regular column for *Custom Home* magazine.

Steve has been a major contributor to the development of the NAHB Chart of Accounts and has lectured frequently for numerous national, state, and local trade associations. He has written articles on the topics of financial management and computerization.

Steve holds an MBA degree in accounting from Rutgers University and a B.A. from Dickinson College. He is a member of the American Institute of Certified Public Accountants.

Mike Benshoof

Mike Benshoof has 14 years of home building and remodeling experience. He is vice president of Steve Maltzman & Associates.

Previously, he was the financial research manager for NAHB's Business

Management Department and served as director of business analysis for NAHB's Economics Group.

Mike was the lead researcher and author of the 2001 edition of the *Cost of Doing Business Study for Home Builders,* the 2001 edition of the *Production Builders Compensation Study,* and the 2001 edition of the *Remodelers Compensation Study.* He has published several articles in home building trade journals.

Mike started his career working for the family building business as a teenager. After college, he joined NVR, Inc., (one of the nation's largest publicly traded home builders), where he spent three years in production and another three years in new-home sales.

While in graduate school, he spent two years with Fannie Mae as an intern specializing in knowledge management.

Mike is a graduate of Penn State University and earned his MBA with a concentration in financial management from Marymount University.

About the NAHB Business Management & Information Technology Committee

The National Association of Home Builders (NAHB) is a Washington-based trade association representing more than 205,000 members involved in home building, remodeling, multifamily construction, property management, subcontracting, design, housing finance, building product manufacturing, and other aspects of residential and light commercial construction.

The Standing Committee on Business Management & Information Technology has jurisdiction over matters relating to improving the business management skills of builder members to enhance their competitiveness, profitability, and professionalism. In accordance with the objectives of the NAHB strategic plan, the committee shall make policy recommendations on business management issues, develop educational programs, write and publish manuals, conduct business management research, and provide consulting assistance to other committees.

Acknowledgments

NAHB's Business Management & Information Technology Committee gratefully acknowledges the individuals who contributed to the *Custom Builder's Business Plan Kit,* which was the inspiration for *Business Plan Guide.*

We would like to thank:

Carol Baye, Custom Construction Concepts, Austin, TX
Allan Brandt, Bainbridge, Inc., Englewood, CO
Patrick Carmichael, Carmichael & Dame Builders, Stafford, TX
Robert Dame, Carmichael & Dame Builders, Stafford, TX
Jack Drake, Drake Homes, Phoenix, AZ
Lee Evans, Lee Evans Group, Littleton, CO
Wayne Foley, W.M. Foley Construction, Great Falls, VA
Steve Hays, Rubin Brown Gornstein & Co., St. Louis, MO
Steve Maltzman, Steve Maltzman & Associates, Redlands, CA
Dennis Marshall, Marshall Building Enterprises, Littleton, CO
Mark Mercurio, Mercurio Homes, Cincinnati, OH
Vernon Palmer, Palmer Homes, Bend, OR
John Piazza, Piazza Construction, Mount Vernon, WA
Randy Rinehart, Rinehart Homes, Charlottesville, VA
John Stout, J. Stout and Associates, Williamsburg, VA
Bob Whitten, Land Solutions, Ft. Myers, FL

Book Production

Business Plan Guide: Simple Steps to Building Business Plans was produced under the general direction of Gerald Howard, NAHB Executive Vice President and CEO, in association with NAHB staff members Michael Shibley, Executive Vice President, Builder, Associate, and Affiliate Services; Greg French, Staff Vice President, Publications and Non-dues Revenues; Eric Johnson, Publisher, BuilderBooks; Theresa Minch, Executive Editor; and Jessica Poppe, Assistant Editor.

Contents

APPENDIX

How to Use the Business Plan Guide CD

The compact disk that accompanies this book contains the NAHB Chart of Accounts in Microsoft® Word 2000 format. It also contains a series of financial spreadsheets that are designed to work with Microsoft® Excel versions 97, 2000, and XP. Use the NAHB Chart of Accounts and the financial spreadsheets to prepare the financial section of your business plan. Please refer to Section Six, Financial Plan, for a detailed explanation of how to use these tools.

The compact disc will automatically start when you insert it into your CD-ROM drive. Click on the links to view the files in a browser. To alter the files, open Microsoft® Word or Excel and then open the corresponding files on the disk using that application. Save the files on your computer's hard drive. If you encounter technical problems, consult the user's manual for the application.

BUSINESS PLANNING

Introduction

Over the years, the building industry has experienced increased competition. Emerging market forces make it harder than ever for builders to survive. That's why you can no longer rely solely on your skills as a craftsman to make it as a builder. Only those who are prepared to meet the challenges of the marketplace will continue to prosper in the future. But how do you beat the odds in an ever-changing environment?

The Business Plan

The key to success lies in organization and planning. Effective planning involves establishing goals, developing strategies, setting priorities, and evaluating results. The *Business Plan Guide* is designed to guide you through the process of developing a business plan.

This kit contains six sections. The overview explains the planning process, including who in the company should be involved in business planning, key areas that should be addressed in every business plan, guidelines for planning, and pointers for monitoring your results. The first section describes how to write an executive summary; you'll actually complete this step after you've written the rest of your business plan. The second section asks you a series of questions to evaluate your company's current structure and operations; it's important groundwork for planning where you want to go and how you should get there. The third, fourth, fifth, and sixth sections guide you through the process of creating your own business plan. You'll develop a plan of action for every aspect of your business, including sales and marketing, production, customer satisfaction, and financial management.

This kit is designed to help you become a more effective manager and to improve your company's productivity and long-term profitability. To get the maximum benefit of this kit, before beginning the planning exercises it is important to understand what a business plan is and how it can benefit you.

A business plan is simply an operating tool that helps you manage your company more effectively. It eliminates the uneasiness and uncertainty associated with flying by the seat of your pants. Functioning as a road map, the business plan outlines where you want the company to go, how you intend to get it there, and what it will look like when it arrives.

The business plan sets standards, defines expected results, guides the operation of the business over a specified period of time, and establishes criteria for measuring performance. The plan provides a focus for management and employees alike; it clearly spells out the role each individual or division in the company plays in achieving the company's common goals. The plan makes everyone in the firm, and ultimately the company itself, more productive and successful.

The Benefits of Planning

Business planning forces you to evaluate your business as it relates to the competitive environment, to develop strategies to overcome possible pitfalls, to set priorities based on long- and short-range goals, and to create action plans. In addition, it offers the following advantages:

- Minimizes the potential for surprises and crises, and prepares you to handle problems more effectively if they arise.
- Helps you identify your resources and determine staffing requirements.
- Encourages employees to work together, under the same directive, toward a common goal.
- Establishes the foundation for better time management. Setting priorities enables you to use your human and material resources most efficiently. The way you manage your resources can significantly impact your company's success.
- Indicates to outside lenders, investors, and customers that you know what you are doing and have a plan to make a profit.
- Saves you money and time by focusing your thinking, and helps you establish a realistic business strategy by giving you more control over your finances, marketing, and daily operations.
- Creates an opportunity for you to build your business on paper before putting your ideas to work in the field. Planning allows you to consider several different scenarios for future action and to examine how each scenario might affect your operation. Identifying potential

challenges may help you to deal with them more effectively or possibly eliminate them completely.

Managing a business without a good financial and business planning system is like playing the game without keeping score. You never know if you are winning, losing, making progress, making an adequate profit, or simply marking time. Maximizing your profits requires a well prepared, well executed financial and business strategy. Planning is the key. Now let's get started.

The Planning Process and the 10 P's

A business plan contains 10 essential components known as the "10 P's," which are outlined below. Identifying these components provides a framework for writing a business plan.

- **Perception–Mission Statement**
  Mission statements generally talk about what the company does, whom it serves, where it is going, and most importantly what makes it special.
- **Purpose–Objectives**
  Objectives are statements about what the company is trying to accomplish.
- **People–Key Personnel**
  Recognizing the strengths and weaknesses of the key people in your organization is essential to writing a business plan. These people will help you implement your plan.
- **Product**
  Understanding whom you build for, what you build, and where you build are integral to developing the plan.
- **Pride–Strengths**
  What is it that differentiates your company from its competitors? Good planning leverages your strengths.
- **Periphery–External Factors**
  Identifying factors outside your company that can make it difficult to accomplish your goals will help you head off problems those factors might impose on your business.
- **Profit–Financial**
  Developing a financial game plan that includes an operating budget and systems to monitor your results is one of the key components of a business plan.

- **Proposals–Goals**
  Goals are what you propose and try to achieve. You need to define realistic and specific goals for all areas of your organization.
- **Pursuit–Strategies**
  Once goals have been set, develop a plan of action for achieving them.
- **Progress–Monitoring Your Plan**
  Put procedures in place to monitor your progress toward accomplishing the goals and objectives developed in your plan.

A Special Note About Goals

If you set goals without doing the necessary legwork–that is, without evaluating your present operations and identifying what you'd like to do in the future–they won't benefit you or your company. Make goal setting fruitful, not frustrating, by keeping the following principles in mind. Effective goals should be:

- **Realistic**
  Make sure what you're aiming for is attainable. It may take some hard work to reach your goals, but don't set yourself up to fail by setting goals you can't possibly achieve.
- **Specific**
  Always tie your goals to a particular function, such as increasing sales or decreasing the number of items on your punch lists. A goal like "Do better next year" is not very helpful.
- **Measurable**
  Make sure your goals are quantifiable. That way, you'll know if you're achieving them or not. For instance, if your goal was to build and close six houses during the next year and at the end of that year you had built and closed eight, you would have exceeded your goal. On the other hand, if you'd only built two and you hadn't closed on either, you would have fallen short of your goal. If you don't meet a goal, you probably need to take a closer look at your operation. Is there something that you could have done differently to have achieved that goal, or is the goal of building six houses simply unrealistic?
- **Within a time frame**
  Set a date by which each of your goals should be met. Some goals are short-term (e.g., complete all warranty items for the Jones family within the next three days), and some are set over a longer term

(e.g., build and close six custom homes over the next 12 months). All goals must have a deadline so you can evaluate whether or not they have been achieved. Goal deadlines are particularly helpful when you are ready to prioritize your tasks.

- **Worthwhile**
  Try to set goals that have clearly defined benefits. If you need to replace your truck, purchasing a new truck within the next month is probably a worthwhile goal. A goal of replacing a one-year-old blue truck with a brand-new red one simply because you like red better is not a worthwhile goal.

Re-evaluation and goal setting should be done on a regular basis. Set goals for each week, month, quarter, year, and for the long term, which for most builders is generally three to five years ahead. Reviewing your written goals reminds you of your objectives and keeps you focused on what needs to be accomplished. In addition, periodic review gives you the opportunity to revise your goals to reflect your accomplishments and to adjust to changes in the marketplace and within your organization.

Put Your Goals Into Action

Once you've set your goals, develop strategies for accomplishing them. Following are some examples of strategies for accomplishing some of a building company's goals.

Goal:
Obtain 10 projects during the year in which we are the only bidder.

Strategy:
Develop a marketing program geared towards obtaining referrals.

Goal:
Increase gross profit by 2 percent in the current year.

Strategies:
Raise markup from 20 percent to 22 percent.
Implement a purchase order system.

After you've developed strategies, write an action plan for accomplishing them. Do this by identifying specific tasks to accomplish the goal, choosing people to do those tasks, assigning responsibilities, and establishing a timetable in which the goals should be accomplished. Following is a hypothetical plan of action for hiring a new field supervisor. This plan is highly detailed for the task at hand. Some tasks require this level of detail; others require less detail.

Goal:
Hire a new field supervisor in one month

Plan of action:

1. Bill will place an ad in the local paper by April 12.
2. If the office staff doesn't receive any ad replies by April 18, they will notify Bill. He will then post employment ads on the bulletin boards at the local lumberyards.
3. The office staff will collect and screen all resumes/job applications and give them to Bill to review by April 28.
4. Bill will select the top five candidates.
5. The office staff will call these candidates by April 29 to set up interviews for May 2.
6. Bill will conduct interviews with the five candidates on May 2.
7. Bill will make his decision by May 5. That day he will call the selected candidate to make a job offer.
8. By May 8, the office staff will send letters to the four other candidates to let them know the position has been filled.
9. The new field supervisor will start work on or before May 8.

Who Should be Involved in Planning?

In a small company, the owner(s) should control the planning process. The owners must determine the general direction in which they want the company to move and must establish the major goals. Good planning must start at and be completely supported by the top. All key individuals in the organization must be involved in and committed to the planning process. The entire management team must feel that they are part of the effort. After all, since they will be the ones implementing the plan, its success (or failure) is riding on them. It is unlikely that forcing your ideas on your staff will generate the same level of commitment that you have. Every person in the company should understand the plan and have his or her own personal plan for meeting the goals for which he or she is responsible.

Some builders have found that working with an advisory group makes business planning easier. These groups are generally made up of individuals who are knowledgeable about sound management practices and are willing to share their time and expertise. Advisors can be other successful business people in the area–possibly your banker or lender, your attorney, your accountant, or business consultants familiar with the home building industry.

Advisory groups give members the opportunity to get together and share their ideas. They have frank discussions about their companies' current situations, what they would like to accomplish in the future, and economic and industry factors that could positively and negatively impact their progress. The group can offer solutions to problems members face and can provide guidance on how to improve their businesses.

These groups typically meet between one and four times a year or more often if the group deems it appropriate. Advisors may also be available for telephone discussions and individual meetings if necessary. NAHB's Builder 20 Clubs facilitate networking among members to help them improve their operations and increase their bottom lines. Log onto www.nahb.org or call 800-368-5242 to find out how to join.

How to Plan

When you sit down to plan, remember that you can't do it all at once. Annual or semi-annual planning meetings help focus on the critical issues at hand and get key employees involved in the process, but planning should not stop there. It's a continuous activity. Some builders believe that planning is actually more effective if they do a little at a time.

No matter how you decide to plan, make it a habit and do it on a regular basis. Dedicate some quiet time each day–15 to 30 minutes or so–to working on your plan. During this quiet time, plan what you are going to do today and for the rest of the week. Then look at this month, this quarter, and the rest of the year. Planning can be a time-consuming process, so make sure you plan time to plan. But don't let yourself get consumed by the planning process; plan some time for your personal life as well.

By now you should have a basic understanding of what planning is and the purpose of doing it. Before moving on to the section where you will actually develop your own business plan, let's take a brief look at the elements that will help make your plan work for you.

Monitoring the Plan

Developing a system to monitor the progress of your business plan is as important as the plan itself. You need to compare your company's actual results to your plan on a timely basis. Measurement systems must be both financial and non-financial. From a financial point of view, it's vital to regularly compare your operating budget to your actual results. Non-financial goals should also be monitored regularly to identify areas where you are falling short of your goals. Once you have completed your plan, it should become an essential working document for the years to come. The plan should not be static; it's a dynamic document that should be modified to accommodate changes in your environment.

Following are some items to monitor on a regular basis:

Income Statement Highlights

- Include month-to-date and year-to-date totals
- Include budget and actual amounts
- Identify each category as a percentage of sales
- Report on the following main categories:
  - Sales and gross profit for each main category of work performed
  - Overhead expense by major category

Detail Operating Expenses

- Include month-to-date and year-to-date totals
- Include budget and actual amounts
- Identify expenses as a percentage of sales

Summarized Job Analysis

- Separate completed jobs from work in progress
- Include original contract, change orders, costs to date, costs to complete, billings to date, revenue earned, over (under) billings, and gross profit remaining.

Balance Sheet Highlights

- Include columns for current month, prior month, and changes. Report on the following accounts:
  - Cash
  - Accounts receivable
  - Accounts payable
  - Other current liabilities
  - Working capital (current assets/current liabilities)
  - Changes in fixed assets, notes, and other accounts

Key Ratios

- Monitor monthly changes and identify trends
- Working capital ratio (current assets/current liabilities)
- Debt-to-equity ratio (total liabilities/total equity)
- Months of overhead covered (operating expenses compared to gross profit remaining on jobs in progress)

Plan Details

To ensure that your plan is functional and that you can evaluate your progress at each step in the planning process, it is essential that you document the following:

Identify the results you want and expect. Write them down. If you can't state your objectives clearly, you may not truly know what you want to accomplish. Here are some examples of desired results: 1) Build more houses, 2) increase net profit, 3) add one more field supervisor, and 4) finish the Evergreen Road project.

Set priorities. Don't try to accomplish everything at once. Look at all of your tasks and determine which ones must be completed most urgently. Concentrate on these items first. Identify items that must be addressed in the near future and those that can wait until a later date. Attempting to complete all tasks simultaneously is nearly impossible and may prevent you from reaching *any* of your goals.

Set goals for priority items. As mentioned previously, goals must be realistic, measurable, specific, accomplishable within a time frame, and worthwhile. In addition, they must identify who, where, what, when, why, and how. For instance, the specific goals that would produce the above-mentioned results may include: 1) Build and close three more homes this year than last year, 2) increase net profit from 8 percent to 20 percent this year, 3) add one more field supervisor in one month, and 4) finish the Evergreen Road project by July 15. This way, you can measure your actual results against your desired results to determine if you are meeting your expectations.

Develop a plan of action. Without a written plan of action, goals are little more than wishes. Understand how each goal affects the others. Identify obstacles and find ways to avoid them. Be prepared. Recognize potential problems and consider alternate solutions so that you can take immediate action should those problems arise.

Areas to Be Included in the Business Plan

The elements of the plan should include all of the areas that are important to the success of your business, including sales, production, financial management, human resources, and administrative issues. The components listed above should be included in your business plan. This list, however, is not comprehensive. It's simply an outline of the general areas you should plan. You may identify additional areas not listed here that are pertinent to your operation, so plan for them as well. If something directly affects your business, it should be accounted for in your business plan.

As you plan each area, remember to specify your expected results, both short- and long-range, based on what you want to accomplish.

Conclusion

Your introduction to business planning is now complete. You should have all the tools you need to move ahead into the following sections to build a plan of your own. If you would like more information on business planning or want to learn about other topics discussed in this section, please see the list of recommended readings in the appendix on page 61.

As you undertake the planning process, keep in mind that business planning, like any new skill, takes some time to master. Don't expect to write the perfect plan on your first try. Some words of advice: Keep your plan simple and straightforward. Just include the most important items first. As you get more experienced at planning, you can expand from there.

Use common sense and don't get lost in the details. Keep your eye on your target and continue to plan on a regular basis. Before you know it, planning will become second nature to you. It will become an integral part of your business, that, like e-mail and automatic teller machines, you won't know how you ever managed without.

Section One

EXECUTIVE SUMMARY

Although this section is the first one in the plan, it is actually the last section to be written. The executive summary should be written when your entire plan is in its draft stages. This section should include your business plan's highlights and key issues. The executive summary should be geared to address the specific needs and interests of people who read your plan. Try to keep the executive summary to two pages or less.

Here is an example of an executive summary from a home builder's business plan:

Business Plan for Smith Homes, Inc., 2003

Executive Summary

Smith Homes, Inc., is a small-volume residential construction company that builds custom and speculative homes. Its corporate offices are located at 12 Main Street, Any Town, Any State, 00000.

Smith Homes, Inc., was established as an S Corporation on January 15, 1985. President and CEO John Smith is the only employee. The company's sales and administrative offices are located in the owner's home.

Smith Homes, Inc., builds luxury homes within a 25-mile radius of Any Town, Any State. The company offers one-of-a-kind homes, top-notch customer service, individual Web pages so customers can track their homes' progress online, and flexible office hours to suit its customers' needs.

Our current and potential customers primarily consist of corporate, medical, and academic professionals and a few retirees. Some are move-up buyers; others are empty nesters. They range in age from 33 to 70.

Our mission is to build homes of extraordinary quality and unique design that exceed our customers' expectations. Our main objective is to build a strong referral base by dedicating ourselves to our customers. Our goal is steady income through continual growth. We plan to build two to three houses a year.

Overhead is $128,000 a year. Selling one home a year at $700,000, excluding land, with a gross profit of 28 percent will achieve a 10 percent net profit.

Loans from the owner provide funding for the company's spec homes. Financing for the custom homes is funded through construction loans customers obtain from several local lenders.

PRESENT STATUS

You can't build a house without materials. Likewise, you can't write a business plan without a clear, accurate picture of your company's history and the status of your current operations.

Section Two, Present Status, asks you detailed questions about your company's purpose, or mission, your organizational structure, and your employees. The answers to these questions will form a foundation on which your operating plan will be built. In the next sections, you'll set goals and strategies for your marketing and sales function, production planning and control, customer satisfaction, and financial management.

You may find that not all questions apply to your operation. In this case, simply answer the questions that directly relate to what you *are* doing (or what you *should* be doing). All answers should be completed in writing, reviewed regularly, and compared to your company's actual results.

How to Complete These Exercises

We recommend spending approximately one week working on each step in the planning process. At least once a week, go back and review the previously completed steps. Make any necessary updates or modifications. After all of the steps are completed and documented, review them from start to finish and begin to implement your plan. Be sure to record and evaluate your progress at least once a month.

Mission Statement

Identify your company's vision by expressing it in a mission statement. Mission statements generally state what a company does, whom it serves, and what makes it special. They should be short (a few sentences at most) and should be written in layman's terms so that anyone–including people outside your company–can understand them. Here are some sample mission statements from home building companies:

ABC Custom Builders creates handcrafted homes for the discerning buyer. We achieve this through the hard work of the most experienced employees in the industry. ABC Custom Builders has been building these homes since 1980 and will maintain this formula for success to ensure our customers have someone to rely on when they are ready for their next home.

EFG Builders encourages dreams, relationships, and opportunities. Our extraordinary team members are passionate about exceeding expectations in design, style, value, and customer satisfaction.

HIJ Builders strives to be recognized as a professional, high-quality, and ethical home building company. We make sure the company runs smoothly and efficiently so that our clients always receive timely, on-budget, and beautiful homes. We work to be the employer of choice, and by doing so, have a team of loyal and highly skilled employees and trade contractors. We work towards an ultimate goal for every client: We become "Your Contractor for Life."

Here are some questions and pointers to help you write your mission statement:

1. Describe the values and business principles that underlie your work. Think about what sets you apart from your competitors.
2. What needs or opportunities does your company serve? Your answer should include a brief description of the types of products you build.
3. How does your company address those needs? Briefly describe how you build and/or remodel those projects.
4. What types of customers do you build them for?
5. Briefly describe your company's financial success.

Company Philosophy

If someone asks you, "Why are you in business?" your answer will reflect your company's philosophy. It's different from your mission statement in that it describes your company's purpose. The former describes "what"; the latter describes "why."

1. What business are you in?
2. What is the purpose of your business?
3. Why are you in business?

4. Describe your company as you want others in the community to think about it.
5. How do you want your customers to feel about your company?

Company History

In this section you examine where your company's been. This will help you define what you'd like to achieve in the future. Take an inventory of your company's history by answering the following questions:

1. When was your company founded?
2. Who founded it?
3. Where was your company founded?
4. How many projects did you build and/or remodel the first year you were in business?
5. What was the dollar volume of your projects the first year you were in business?
6. How many projects did you build and/or remodel last year?
7. What are some challenges your company has overcome?

Organizational Structure

An organizational chart illustrates a company's structure. It's useful for explaining how each function (position) in the organization relates to other functions. Put one together for your company by completing these exercises:

1. Draw a box at the top of a blank piece of paper (you can do this with computer software, too). Put the top executive's (the owner, for example) job title in the box.
2. Below that box, draw boxes for company executives who report to that person. Put their titles and the divisions, units, departments, etc., they're in charge of in the boxes.
3. Below those boxes, draw boxes for managers who report to those executives. Include their titles, as well as the divisions, units, departments, etc., they're in charge of in the boxes.

Keep drawing boxes and adding titles and departments until you've accounted for every position in the company. Here's a sample organizational chart:

EFG Builders

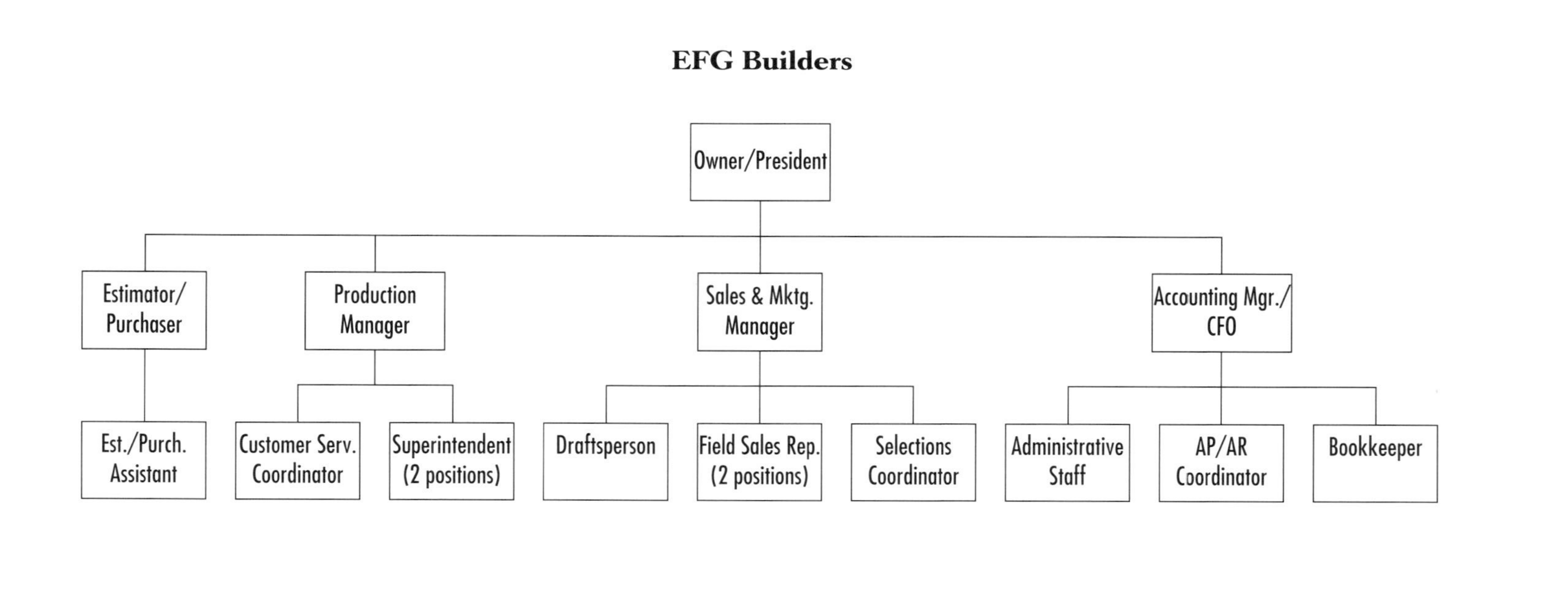

You should have a written job description for every position in your chart. After you've developed your organizational chart, answer these questions:

1. How do you want your employees to view you as a boss?
2. What position(s) should be cut if there is a downturn?
3. Do you have a personnel budget? If so, please attach it.

Before answering the following questions, take a look at your growth plans for the next three to five years. See the financial plan in Section Six.

1. What additional staffing requirements do you anticipate in order to meet your projected volume?
2. Why do you need these additional employees?
3. Where will any additional staff come from?
4. What training and coaching will they need?

Employees

An effective business plan requires a team that buys into the plan and works to make it happen. Lay the groundwork for that buy-in by assessing every employee's current tasks to see what additional responsibilities they can take on. Assess their strengths and weaknesses, too, to see if they need training.

Using the organizational chart you created in the last step, list every employee in the company. For each person, answer the following questions and complete these exercises:

1. Attach the employee's resume.
2. What has this employee accomplished in the past?
3. What are this employee's strengths?
4. What can be done to take advantage of his or her strengths?
5. How can he or she improve in the future? Set goals for this person (i.e., become more computer literate; communicate more effectively with others), as well as strategies and an action plan for accomplishing the goals.
6. What training and coaching will be needed?
7. What additional tasks can this employee take on?
8. How is this employee compensated? (Include salary, commission, benefits, etc.)
9. Is it the most effective form of compensation for top performance?

DEVELOPING THE PLAN

The present status assessment you did in Section Two lays the groundwork for the next task at hand: writing your business plan.

As we mentioned in the introduction, you can't do business planning all at once. It's best to do it a little at a time and to work on one part at a time. Likewise, you can't write a business plan all at once or you'll leave out important parts and steps.

An effective business plan contains separate plans for each part of your business. First, you'll lay the groundwork for your sales and marketing plan by analyzing your market and product. You'll set goals and strategies for your sales and marketing function, and then move on to production, customer satisfaction, and your financial plan.

After you've written separate plans for each part of your business, you'll be ready to write your business plan's executive summary. But don't stop there. Your work isn't finished. Keep your plan active by regularly comparing your goals, strategies, and action plans to your actual results. Review the monitoring suggestions in the introduction. If you find yourself falling short of your goals, adjust your plan accordingly.

Section Three

SALES AND MARKETING PLAN

There are many things to consider when developing a comprehensive marketing plan. The task can take some time, but the payoff is well worth it down the road. A good sales and marketing plan can help prevent sleepless nights and can help keep your company focused.

There are eight key areas to research and analyze for an effective sales and marketing plan: economic, regulatory, technological, competition, customer, product and land, lead generation, and settlement or draw coordination. Then two last steps in this section help you systematize your sales process and tie the plan together.

Economic Analysis

With so many things competing for your time, it's hard to keep up with a subject you may not understand well or even want to understand well. However, comprehending the local and national economy is one of the most effective ways to help you make better business decisions.

For example, changes in monthly payroll employment numbers are key indicators of the likely course of housing demand. They should be compared to the rate of change for your local market in the past few years, and to the rates of change in other regions and for the nation as a whole. Payroll employment data also should be compared to the number of housing permits relative to your area's population.

The NAHB Economics Group is one of the best resources for practical, easy-to-understand information about the economy. Much of its information, including statistics on metropolitan area employment and permits, is available on the Web at www.nahb.org. The NAHB Economics Group also offers several excellent publications containing more in-depth information, such *Home Builders Forecast, Housing Market Statistics,* and *Housing Economics.*

1. What's the current economic state of your market? Is it healthy or declining?
2. What's the short- and long-term economic outlook for your market?
3. What economic factors may impact your market? (e.g., large employers moving into or out of the area, tax incentives granted to build certain types of housing, rising lumber costs, etc.)
4. Has population been increasing, decreasing, or remaining steady in your market?
5. What are the major companies that your buyers work for?
6. How healthy are those companies? (Have they announced any layoffs or plans for expansion?)
7. How are your market's demographics changing? (e.g., more couples having children, more multi-generational families living in the same households, more people employed by large corporations moving into or out of the area, more people working from home, etc.)
8. How do you think your market's housing needs will change in response to changing demographics?

Regulatory Analysis

Regulatory factors can add thousands of dollars to the cost of building new homes. Unfortunately, it is rare that all of the added costs can be passed on to your buyers. In addition to costs, regulatory factors may prevent you from building the product you need to build. In some cases, they may prevent you from building in a certain area altogether.

It is important to learn who the policy makers in your market are. Get to know them personally, if possible, and track their decisions. Maintaining your NAHB membership and staying active within your local association are some of the best ways to stay informed about policies that may affect your business. The NAHB local and national associations work hard to fight policies that adversely affect the home building industry.

1. How do regulatory factors (e.g., wetlands protection, coastal zoning, local zoning, etc.) affect the homes you build and/or remodel?
2. What future regulatory factors may affect your market in the short- and long-term?

Technological Analysis

Today's consumers are more demanding than ever when it comes to technology factors. Some people even make buying decisions based on the technology offered within a community and within your homes. Make sure you offer the technology your customers are looking for. That doesn't always mean you have to offer the latest technological fad, but you must pay attention to available technology.

Some technologies offer builders an excellent opportunity to increase margins, but only if you offer the technology buyers want and are willing to pay for.

1. What technological factors (e.g., broadband access, fiber-optic availability, etc.) affect the homes you build?
2. What future technological factors may affect your market in the short and long term?

Competition Analysis

It's important to know how your competitors operate. You need to get out and shop the competition often. Don't just visit their model homes; drive their jobsites, too. Many of the following questions should be answered at least quarterly but preferably monthly. If you have a sales staff, explain the key criteria you are looking for and have them analyze the competition for you.

When possible, obtain marketing brochures from your competitors and keep them on file. Pay attention to items like new pricing, new product types, new sections of a community opening, etc. Keep copies of your competitors' local media advertisements. Pay attention to your competitors' sales pace, especially when they run major ongoing marketing campaigns.

1. List your competitors and answer the following questions for each:
   a) What is their mission statement and/or company goals?
   b) Approximately how many homes or communities did they sell in the past year?
   c) What type of homes do they sell?
   d) What was their average sales price?
   e) Approximately how many homes did they sell within each community?
   f) What was the average sales price within each community?
   g) What is your competitor known for within your market?
   h) What does your competitor do better than you?
   i) What do you do better than your competitor?
   j) How do/can you differentiate yourself from this competitor? (past and future)

2. Did any of your competitors go out of business within the last year? If so, why?
3. What can you learn from your competitors (including former ones that are no longer operating)?
4. If more competitors start doing business in your area, what can you do to protect your market share?
5. What is the resale market like in your market?
6. How many homes on the market are within your price range?
7. How many days are they on the market?
8. Are the listing price and the closing price the same or less? (It's worth the effort to compare county records with MLS info.)

Customer Analysis

You can't close a home without a customer. That statement may seem obvious, but many builders don't obtain enough information about their customers. The result is often severe. Customer analysis is one of the most crucial aspects of your business. If you don't offer the things buyers look for, you won't survive. Know your customers!

Getting to know your customers depends on gathering as much information as you can about them. The questions below will help you do that. Don't make assumptions about your customers; if you are wrong, it could be costly. There are several places to find out hard data about your market place such as the U.S. Census Bureau and economic and market analysis companies. Your local business bureau may also have information about consumers.

Once you find out who lives in your market, you can design your product to suite their needs or look at other potential markets you may want to consider.

1. Describe typical or potential customers by answering these questions about them:
   a) What is the average household income of my buyer?
   b) What is the age of the primary buyer?
   c) What is the family makeup (e.g., children, parents, special ethnic considerations, etc.)
   d) What do they do for a living? (are they engineers, doctors, managers, etc.)
2. How many potential buyers are in your market, and how do you know this?

3. What customer needs/wants/desires will your homes satisfy?
4. Are your home sites in a desirable location?
5. What lifestyle choices do your homes satisfy? (e.g., good school system, close to recreation, convenient location, close to urban areas, rural areas, etc.)
6. Are your homes the best size (sq. ft.) and design for the market?
7. Are you a price leader or a value leader?
8. What features do you offer that your customers want? (e.g., extra bedrooms, entertainment rooms, upgraded kitchens, home offices, etc.)

The following questions and answers will be used to develop your overall customer satisfaction plan in Section Five. Answer these questions in regards to sales only. You will be asked a series of questions about production in Section Four and you will combine them into one cohesive plan in Section Five.

1. What is your overall sales and marketing customer satisfaction plan? Start with the initial customer contact and explain the techniques used by the sales department to achieve ultimate service until settlement.
2. How do you measure customer satisfaction?
3. How do you make good use of the results to manage future business decisions?
4. How do you manage customer expectations? (e.g., do you have written specifications you show your customer? Are your contracts clear? Do you focus on areas that have been problematic in the past?)

Product and Land Analysis

Understanding your customer well makes product analysis much easier. Once you know what your customer wants, you can establish a plan to build the most profitable homes that suit their needs.

An in-depth look at marketing product analysis is not complete until you compare the results with financial marketing analysis. A marriage that makes your best-selling homes your most profitable homes is most desirable and is possible with careful planning and analysis.

The first step is to define the products you currently offer and those you plan to offer in the future. The following questions will help you determine your current and potential sales patterns. Later, you'll analyze the profitability of current and future sales patterns. Then, by comparing the two, you can start to develop a strategy that will not only sell homes, but will sell profitable homes.

1. How many home sites do you currently own or have options for? (List the total number, and then break it out by community.)
2. How many home sites will you need next year, in the next three years, and in the next five years to build the number of homes you are projecting?
3. How will you acquire new land?
4. How long will it take before you can build on the land?
5. How much will future land cost?
6. Will major changes in land costs support your current price range and design of homes?
7. Will you need to redesign your product to suit the land costs?
8. What do you build?
9. What is your justification for building each type of product? (e.g., presales, specs, remodeling, etc.)
10. How do you build? (e.g., what portion of your work is done with your own crews?)
11. How do you price your homes?
12. Do you use a standard mark up? If so, what is it?
13. Do you do market analysis pricing?
14. List your plan types and how many of each you sold in the past two or three years. Start with the plan that sold the most homes and end with the one that sold the least. (We will revisit this question in the financial section.)
15. Do you plan on offering any new products (plan types)?
16. When do you plan to offer them?
17. Where do you build?
18. Why did you choose these sites to build?
19. List all the communities (subdivisions) where you are currently building and are committed to build in the future. For each community, supply the following information:
    a) Number of available home sites available to your company. (How many home sites do you own, option, or need to take down?)
    b) What plan type is your model within each community, or what plan type will your model be within future communities?
    c) List other builders within the community. (If there are other

builders within your community, it's imperative to complete the competition analysis each month.)

d) Number of homes you offer within community.
e) Price range of homes.
f) Sizes of homes.
g) Typical buyer or projected buyer profile.

Lead Generation Analysis

No matter how many homes you build and/or remodel, it's important to measure and analyze where your leads and eventual sales come from. To start, you need to figure out how many leads you typically need per eventual sale. Then you need to determine where the best and most numerous leads come from. Merely getting numbers isn't always as important as it is to get quality prospects that turn into sales. Quantity and quality aren't the same thing.

If you have model homes, it's important to use registration cards that ask how potential customers found you. Make sure you have buyers fill out a marketing survey asking them to rank the top sources that got them in your door. Measure these results against the overall lead data. Make sure you also ask them to rank the top reasons they purchased from you. You can use that data to learn more about who your customers are.

If you're a smaller volume or custom builder, get in the habit of asking leads how they found out about you. Keep a short written questionnaire by the phone and make it a habit to get the information every time.

Once you have the survey information, don't let it collect dust. Measure the response frequency often. Note spikes resulting from increased marketing efforts during the year. And track response trends during different times of the year. Once you have year-over-year data, start comparing different times of the year with each other.

Survey work is tricky. It's easy to inadvertently design a cumbersome form or to write badly worded questions that make your data inaccurate and potentially useless. Consider hiring a professional to help you design an effective survey and help you analyze the data.

1. How many sales did you have last year?
2. How many leads/prospects did you have last year?
3. What is your sales-to-leads ratio? Compare sales to leads, such as 5 sales to 100 leads, and then divide total sales by total leads to determine ratio. For example, 5/100 = .05, or a 5 percent conversion ratio.

4. How many leads and sales did you get from the following advertising venues? (Use the worksheets on the next page to analyze leads and sales for the entire company, for larger builders, and then by individual communities.)
5. What can you do to attract more qualified leads?
6. What will it take to sell and close your current and newly generated leads?
7. What can you do to increase your sales-to-leads ratio?
8. Who sells your product?
9. What can they do better?
10. How can/will you work with brokers and Realtors?
11. How does your referral program work?
12. If you don't have a referral program, how will you implement one this year?

Settlement or Draw Coordination Analysis

This is one of those points of contact with customers that can turn into a disaster if not managed carefully. Most builders aren't large enough to own their own in-house mortgage and title company. Even if they are, it's difficult to capture every customer in house. So, what happens to a typical builder when he or she has to depend on outside lenders and title companies, or banks if the customer is financing the home? Many times, all goes smoothly. However, when things do go wrong with draws and settlements, they really go wrong. Even if the mortgage company, title company, or bank is in the wrong, the customer *will blame you.* After all, you're the one building the home.

Good builders put measures in place to resolve problems. Great builders put preventative measures in place to avoid problems in the first place.

Settlements

Please keep in mind that the settlement process is not just the "closing day." It's actually the entire process, from loan application to closing. The following questions will help you develop a critical settlement path from sale to closing or final draw. Use your answers to determine where you can make process improvements.

1. How many different companies (e.g., mortgage companies, title companies, law firms) do you work with on the path to settlement?

Company-Wide Leads and Sales

Source	Leads	Sales
Newspaper		
Direct mail		
Internet		
Homeowner referrals		
Other referrals		
Realtors		
Architects		
Billboards		
Signage		
Additional sources		

XYZ Community Analysis

Source	Leads	Sales
Newspaper		
Direct mail		
Internet		
Homeowner referrals		
Other referrals		
Realtors		
Architects		
Billboards		
Signage		
Additional sources		

2. What percentage of closings is each company involved in?
3. Describe your comfort level with each of the companies you work with frequently. (e.g., Do they have good customer service for you and the customer? Are they efficient? Do they make mistakes often? Do they correct errors promptly?)
4. What are some of the typical problems that arise with customers or mortgage/title firms prior to or at settlement?
5. What things typically upset customers during the settlement process?
6. How can you or the settlement company take corrective action?
7. What can the company do to make the settlement process easier for itself and the customer?
8. What opportunities do you have to impress the customer during the settlement process?
9. How can you work diligently to reduce the number of different mortgage and finance companies you deal with by partnering and offering customers incentives to choose the ones you partner with?

Draws

Your risk exposure goes down when customers finance their own homes, but that doesn't eliminate the possibility of having unhappy customers. Answer these questions to determine how to make your and your customers' dealings with the bank as painless as possible.

1. On average, how many draws do you take on homes?
2. Have you challenged the banks you most frequently work with to increase the number of draws per home?
3. How many different companies do you work with on the draw path?
4. What percentage of home sales is each involved in?
5. Describe your comfort level with each of the companies you work with frequently. (e.g., do they have good customer service for you and the customer? Are they efficient? Do they make mistakes often? Do they correct errors promptly?)
6. What things typically upset customers during the draw distribution process?
7. How can you or the bank take corrective action?
8. How can you work diligently to reduce the number of different banks you deal with by partnering and offering customers incentives to choose the ones you partner with?

Systematizing Your Marketing Plan

Planning is futile if you don't have the proper systems in place to manage, measure, and maintain your sales process. Too many builders don't realize they are behind until the end of the year, and then sacrifice profit to make their plans. The following questions will help you implement an actionable plan.

1. What systems do you use to measure the success of your sales and marketing plan?
2. Where do you need to be each month to make your yearly goals?
3. What are your back-up plans in case you don't make your plan?
4. What are your plans to take advantage of an unexpected hot market? (e.g., do you have systems in place to raise prices if you get ahead of your sales plan so you don't leave money on the table?)

One of the best ways to easily systematize your sales process is to plan each month's sales one year in advance, based on previous sales experience in prior years. If you build in multiple communities, complete this exercise for each community.

The CD that comes with this book includes an Excel spreadsheet for financial planning. Part of the financial template asks for sales forecasting information you can use to plan and measure your sales throughout the year. The same spreadsheet will be used to determine production schedules and needs and will help drive your pro forma budget.

Tying the Plan Together

To make your sales and marketing plan work, you need to complete one more step. Use the answers to the questions above to write a one- or two-page sales and marketing summary that will become a part of your executive summary.

Focus on defining your overall marketing strategy in a few short paragraphs. Then use bullet points to define specific milestones throughout the year. Clearly write out actionable items and indicate who is responsible for ensuring that those items are completed.

Give copies of the summary to all of your employees. Share your goals (especially sales goals) with everyone, from executives to laborers.

Section Four

PRODUCTION PLAN

Now that you have an effective plan in place to market and sell your homes, you must map out a plan to *efficiently* build the homes you sell. You also need to put controls in place that ensure that your company's sales and production departments communicate with each other.

The production process includes six key areas: administration, customer service, quality control, field management, estimating and plans, and purchasing. Each of these areas depends on the other. You must set up each area in a manner that encourages open communication with the other areas.

Administration

Builders often overlook administrative support. Administrators, especially receptionists, tend to have frequent contact with your customers and can be a positive or negative influence upon them. Make sure you hire administrative support personnel who reflect your attitudes towards your customers. It's easy to train administrators, but next to impossible to train attitude or personality.

1. How many administrative positions do you currently have?
2. Are all administrators in the position that best suits them?
3. Will you need to hire any new administrative employees?
4. What will new employees be responsible for?
5. What type of people are you looking for to fill these positions?
6. Can you consolidate any positions among the current administrative staff?
7. What can you do to empower administrators to make good decisions on the company's behalf?

Customer Service

A building company that has outstanding quality control and fantastic customer service typically is profitable and efficient, and sells homes even in a slow market. It is extremely difficult to achieve high results in any of these categories without doing everything else well.

As a builder, you have many opportunities to impress your customers. Unfortunately, you also have many opportunities to fall short, and that's what customers remember. Communicating effectively with your customers and delivering a consistent, high-quality product are two great ways to keep them happy.

The following questions will help you develop a plan for achieving high marks with your customers during and after construction. Answer these questions specifically about production. You will use these responses in conjunction with the customer satisfaction questions in Section Three to develop your overall customer satisfaction plan in Section Five.

1. What are your points of contact with a customer? (e.g., product selection, pre-groundbreaking meetings, pre-drywall meetings, walk-throughs, etc.)
2. How do these points of contact help you build a trusting relationship with your customers?
3. What complaints do you typically hear from your customers?
4. What can you do to change those complaints into praise?
5. What surveys do you use to measure customer satisfaction with your production and customer service functions?
6. How do you use customer survey data to give feedback to your architects/designers, estimators, and production team to improve quality and customer service?
7. How do you manage "after settlement" customer service? (Describe in detail.)
8. What are your customer satisfaction goals for this year?
9. What is your plan to improve customer satisfaction during construction this year?

Quality Control

To achieve high levels of quality control, you need a systematized production process and written performance specifications for trades. Quality should be your company's constant pursuit. Holding your employees and trade contractors to high standards during the construction process lowers callbacks and increases customer satisfaction. Done correctly, quality control yields higher profits over time.

The questions below will help you assess your current quality level and identify areas that need improvement. One of the best ways to make immediate improvements is to take an honest look at your quality issues, work backwards to determine the cause of the problem, and then correct it at the source. Sometimes the solution is as simple as changing a product in the home or changing a single step during the production process.

1. How would you describe your level of quality?
2. How do your customers describe your level of quality?
3. Who oversees your company's production function?
4. Describe your production control and management system.
5. What is your weakest area of quality control?
6. What can you do to make it one of your strongest areas of quality control?
7. Do you have written scopes of work for all trades? If so, attach them to the production section of your business plan.
8. What steps do you use to ensure communication between your customer service and production departments?
9. What steps do you use to ensure communication between sales and production?
10. Do you measure product quality issues as part of your customer service work?
11. What corrective measures do you use for products that don't perform to your standards?

Field Management

It is extremely important to implement a process that involves an over-abundance of communication between the sales staff, back office, and field management. If you wear most or all the hats for your business, you still need to develop a system that helps you manage your production process and that will grow with your company. The following questions will help you understand your current process better and will prompt you to make decisions that will help you improve your current process.

1. Who schedules starts?
2. What is the process for starting a home?
3. Do you start a "for sale" home differently than a speculatively built home?

4. How do your sales and production staffs communicate to take advantage of even-flow production (or "slotting")?
5. What system do you use to ensure that the production department has complete information about each home? (This is especially important when changes occur during construction.)
6. Do your production supervisors know your specifications and scopes of work?
7. What system do you use to ensure that they enforce those specs and scopes?
8. What can you do to improve field check processes?
9. What systems do you use to make sure superintendents inform others about problems such as over-ordering or trade contractor issues?
10. Who are your best supervisors?
11. What can you do to train others to be like them?
12. What systems do you use to make sure the correct materials are delivered to jobsites?
13. What is your jobsite clean-up policy?
14. How is it enforced?
15. Who are your best trade contractors?
16. What trade contractors may need to be replaced?
17. What is your plan to replace them?
18. How well do you communicate with your trade contractors?
19. How can you help your trade contractors become more efficient?

Estimating and Plans

This area is often overlooked. Some builders spend months trying to cut 1 percent from their general and administrative expenses. While it's always good to try to trim the fat from budgets, trimming costs from homes is much more effective.

For example, if you cut $1,000 out of your general and administrative expenses, you've only saved $1,000. However, if you trim $500 from the cost of building a specific home and you build that home three times in one year, you've added $1,500 to your bottom line. If you continually trim building costs for each of your plans, you can significantly boost your bottom line.

That's why a growing company should immediately hire an estimator who understands how to work with sales. He or she can value engineer your homes to make sure they're built to strict budgets and can eliminate things your customers aren't willing to pay for. Good estimators typically more than pay for their own salaries in cost savings alone. If you are a custom builder, a good estimator or estimating process is essential.

1. How do you handle estimating within your company?
2. Do you have a process to continually value engineer your products?
3. How long does it typically take for your company to create an estimate?
4. How can you improve the turnaround time?
5. How accurate are your estimates compared with actual costs?
6. How long does it take your company to process non-standard changes to plans?
7. How many plans do you maintain?
8. Do you have too few or too many?
9. How many years have you been building each product?
10. What can you do to freshen up stale plans?

Purchasing

Estimating and plan review help you cut costs, so think of purchasing as the way to turn those savings in to reality. You can't reap the rewards of good estimating without effectively managing the purchasing of goods and labor. A purchase order system is the only way to maintain tight control over the costs of those items.

The questions below will help you assess how well you manage your costs and help identify areas that need improvement.

1. Do you have written trade contractor/vendor agreements?
2. How often do you review your job cost reports?
3. What steps do you use to improve variances between estimates and actual costs?
4. Do you have written procedures for handling purchase orders for trade contractors and/or vendors? If so, reference them here and attach them to the production section of your business plan.
5. How do your purchase order procedures integrate with your field management function?
6. If you don't have written procedures for handling purchase orders, when and how do you plan to produce them?

7. What can you do to improve your purchase order system in the future?
8. Do you have written procedures for handling change orders? If so, reference them here and attach them to the production section of your business plan.
9. How do your change order procedures integrate with your field management function?
10. If you don't have written procedures for handling change orders, when and how do you plan to produce them?
11. What can you do to improve your change order system?
12. Who is responsible for approving payments to vendors and trade contractors?
13. What system do you use to ensure that payments are made on time?
14. How do you ensure that vendors and trade contractors are only paid for work that is done correctly?

Section Five

CUSTOMER SATISFACTION PLAN

Now that you have a plan in place to achieve high customer satisfaction marks in sales and production, you need to develop a cohesive overall company customer satisfaction plan.

It's important to look at all aspects of customer satisfaction in one common area. This section will help you develop a strategy you can readily copy and use as a manual for company customer satisfaction. You may see some holes in certain areas you weren't aware of; if so, you may need to go back to the sales or production sections and change some of your strategies.

The easiest way to develop a cohesive customer satisfaction plan is to think about your timeline of customer contacts. Start with the message you send potential customers through your various advertising mediums and then progress forward from the first contact with a customer to settlement and beyond. Pull the answers from the previous sections and it should be fairly easy to create one cohesive plan.

1. What is your overall sales and marketing customer satisfaction plan? Start with the initial customer contact and explain the techniques used by the sales and/or customer service department(s) to achieve ultimate service until settlement.
2. How do you measure customer satisfaction?
3. How do you make good use of the results to manage future business decisions?
4. How do you manage customer expectations? (e.g., do you have written specifications you show your customer? Are your contracts clear? Do you focus on areas that have been problematic in the past?)
5. What are your points of contact with a customer? (e.g., product selection, pre-groundbreaking meetings, pre-drywall meetings, walk-throughs, etc.)

6. How do these points of contact help you build a trusting relationship with your customers?
7. What complaints do you typically hear from your customers?
8. What can you do to change those complaints into praise?
9. What surveys do you use to measure customer satisfaction with your production and customer service areas?
10. How do you use customer survey data to give feedback to your architects/designers, estimators, and production team to improve quality and customer service?
11. How do you manage "after settlement" customer service? (Describe in detail.)
12. What are your customer satisfaction goals for this year?
13. What is your plan to improve customer satisfaction during construction this year?

Section Six

FINANCIAL PLAN

Now that you have established written goals and strategies for all areas of your business, you need to develop a financial plan to accomplish those goals and strategies.

Base your financial plan on some financial assumptions, which you'll develop from your answers to the questions in Sections Three through Five. The assumptions should be consistent with and derived from the earlier sections in the plan. Use text bullets to describe key assumptions and place the details in tables.

Your financial plan should also include a detailed operating budget, a cash flow budget (which can be an offshoot of your operating budget), a pro-forma income statement and balance sheet, and key financial ratio goals.

Don't prepare financial projections independently from the rest of the plan. For example, your market research results should flow into your sales projections, which should generate your revenue forecasts. Under no circumstances should you do detailed financial projections and *then* write a plan to suit. By all means, do some high-level financial planning at an early stage to get a feel for the basic figures and sensitivities, but don't let the plan to become a financially driven document without any strong market basis.

Before starting to detail your operating expenses, set some basic goals on the number of houses and/or the dollar volume you want to produce in the year ahead. Establish a target net profit you want to make for your company. Net profit should be calculated after paying yourself a "reasonable" salary for the work you perform for the company. Strive for a net profit between 7.5 and 10 percent of anticipated sales volume. According to NAHB's *2001 Cost of Doing Business Study,* the top 25 percent of builders averaged a net profit of 10.5 percent.

Financial Spreadsheets

We've developed a series of interlinked Excel spreadsheets (which you'll find on the CD that accompanies this book) to help you develop the financial section of your business plan. Here are descriptions of the worksheets (tabs) within the spreadsheet and information on how to use them.

Sales/Starts/Closings: On this worksheet you'll enter the number of units you plan to sell in your next fiscal year for each community or type of construction (e.g., spec, custom with land, custom–no land, remodeling). After identifying your sales goals, project your starts and closings. The worksheet includes space to enter information for up to six different communities or job types. In addition, you can enter the financial assumptions described below. This information will be used to compute your sales, cost of sales, financing, and other information that flows to the income statement worksheet. (You'll find more detail about the sales/starts/closings worksheet on the following pages.)

Operating Expenses: On this worksheet you will develop your operating expense budget. The spreadsheet includes four major categories. It is based upon the NAHB Chart of Accounts, which is included on page 63 in the appendix and on the CD.

Income Statement: On this worksheet you will enter actual results from your prior year'(s) activity. All of the pro forma income statement information, with the exception of other income, is computed from information entered on the other worksheets.

Balance Sheet: On this worksheet you will enter actual results from your prior year(s)' activity. Some of the line items on the pro forma balance sheet are computed from information entered on the other worksheets.

Cash Flow: This worksheet will be used to project your cash flow for the pro forma period. Some of the line items on the cash flow projection are computed from information entered on the other worksheets.

Sales, Starts, and Closings

Sales: Enter the number of units you anticipate selling each month by community/type.

Average Sales Price: Enter the average sales price by community/type. This number is multiplied by the number of units closed to compute total revenue on the income statement.

Average Customer Deposit: This amount is used for computing cash inflows on the cash flow tab.

Average Concession Offered: Enter the average amount of concessions offered to the buyer to sell each house. This amount is used to compute the amount in account 6930, sales concessions, on the operating expense tab.

In-House Commission Rate: This amount is multiplied by the total sales amount to compute the commission expense reflected in account 6040, sales commissions, in-house, on the operating expense tab.

Outside Commission Rate: This amount is multiplied by the total sales amount and the amount entered in the percentage co-op sales line to compute the commission expense reflected in account 6050, sales commissions, outside, on the operating expense tab.

Average Construction Costs: Enter the average direct construction costs by home by community/type. This number is multiplied by the number of units closed to compute total direct construction costs on the income statement.

Average Land Costs: Enter the average land costs by home by community/type. This number is multiplied by the number of units closed to compute total land costs on the income statement.

Average Days Under Construction: Enter the average number of days in your construction cycle. This amount can be used along with the amounts entered as starts, average construction loan commitment, and average interest rate to compute the amount reflected in account 5040, interest incurred during construction, on the operating expense tab.

Construction Loan Fees: Enter the average amount paid in fees on your construction loan for each community/type. This amount can be used to compute the amount reflected in account 5120, points and fees, on the operating expense tab.

Average Appraisal Fee: Enter the average amount paid for each house for each community/type. This amount can be used to compute the amount reflected in account 5130, appraisals and related fees, on the operating expense tab.

Starts: Enter the number of units you anticipate starting each month by community/type. These amounts are used to compute the amount reflected in account 5040, interest incurred during construction, on the operating expense tab.

Closings: Enter the number of units you anticipate closing each month by community/type. This number is multiplied by the average sales price to compute total revenue on the income statement.

Developing Your Operating Budget

When developing their annual operating budgets, many builders identify their annual expenditures and divide that amount by 12 to come up with a monthly operating budget. Using this method doesn't give you a true picture of your monthly operations.

The best way to start developing your operating budget is to review your current year's activity on a month-by-month basis. Identify your fixed expenses (those that won't change with volume) and plan for possible increases. Examine your variable expenses (expenses that vary with changes in volume) and link them to your targeted sales goals.

When preparing your annual budget, try to identify the month in which you'll incur the expenses. For example, when planning the amount you expect to spend for advertising, identify when you plan on running your ads and put the planned expenditures in that particular month. If you place an ad in the Yellow Pages, budget for the cost of the ad in the month when you'll make the expenditure.

We recommend breaking down your operating expenses into four major categories: indirect construction costs, financing expenses, sales and marketing expenses, and general and administrative expenses.

The operating expense tab on the financial spreadsheet lists most of the accounts in the NAHB Chart of Accounts you should use to organize your budget. It is not necessary to use all of the accounts. If you decide not to enter the detail accounts, you can enter the total amount for the category on the category heading line. For example, instead of breaking out warranty costs into account 4710–salaries and wages, warranty; 4720–materials, warranty; 4730–subcontractor, warranty; and 4790–other warranty expenses, you can enter all of the warranty expense by month in the category heading row titled 4700–4790–warranty and customer service.

Indirect Construction Costs

Indirect construction costs include other job-related costs that can't be attributed to a specific unit. Use the answers from the production section of your business plan to identify the monthly costs within this area.

Following are the major categories within the indirect construction costs section of the financial spreadsheet. Refer to the NAHB Chart of Accounts for a more detailed description of the individual accounts in each category.

Salaries and Wages: Include compensation paid to indirect construction personnel including your superintendents, laborers, estimator, production manager, draftsman, and purchasers. Identify the gross wages in the actual month they will be paid (e.g., for weekly payrolls, you will have some months with four weeks and some with five weeks).

We suggest budgeting for your superintendents and laborers as operating expenses. If a superintendent receives a salary, his or her costs are the same whether you build 10 or 12 houses. If you treat the cost of your laborers or superintendents as a direct construction cost, don't include it in the operating budget. Make sure to add these salaries and wages to the direct construction cost line on the sales/starts/closing tab.

Payroll Taxes and Benefits: Include the payroll taxes and benefits relating to indirect construction personnel. You may want to track the payroll taxes and benefits relating to sales personnel within the general and administrative section of the spreadsheet. For payroll taxes, budget for the time when your people go over the tax limits (e.g., federal unemployment taxes are only paid on the first $8,000 of wages. Once the individual reaches $8,000 of wages, unemployment taxes are no longer calculated).

Field Office Expenses: Include all of the costs of your construction office as well as communication costs for your construction personnel.

Field Warehouse and Storage Expenses: Include the costs of renting or owning a warehouse or storage facility.

Construction Vehicles and Equipment: Include all costs relating to operating construction vehicles and equipment. It's generally hard to budget for repairs and maintenance on a monthly basis since you can't predict when your vehicles will break down. Planning for scheduled maintenance on your vehicle is one way of smoothing out the guesswork. In the long run, routine maintenance usually leads to longer vehicle life and less unplanned expenditures.

Expenses for Maintaining Unsold Units: This is the category in which you budget for the expenses for carrying your spec homes after they are completed. Interest on finished inventory is included within the financing expense section.

Warranty and Customer Service: We recommend including warranty costs in this category and not burying them as a job cost.

Depreciation: Include depreciation on construction department vehicles and equipment. You may want to include all of your depreciation expense within the general and administrative category.

Financing Expenses

Following are the major categories within the financing expenses section of the financial spreadsheet. Refer to the NAHB Chart of Accounts for a more detailed description of the individual accounts in each category.

Interest: Include all interest paid, including interest incurred during construction and interest on finished inventory. We recommend treating construction period interest and interest on finished inventory as an operating expense because these expenses have more to do with managing your cash flow overall than relating to a particular home. For example, if you were to build the same plan type at the different times of the year, you may have to draw down on construction loans when building one of the homes. However, you might not need to draw down on your construction loans to build the second home because you previously had a group of closings. When comparing your direct construction costs between the two homes you may be skewing your results if one has interest and the other doesn't.

If you treat construction period interest or interest on finished inventory as a direct construction cost, don't include it in the operating budget. Make sure to add your construction period interest to your direct construction cost line on the sales/starts/closings tab.

Construction Loans–Points and Fees: Include any points and related fees related to your construction loans in this category. If you treat construction loan fees as a direct construction cost, don't include it in the operating budget. Make sure to add your construction period interest to your direct construction cost line on the sales/starts/closing tab.

Closing Costs: Include the costs of closing your construction loans in this category. Closing costs related to settlement of your homes should be included as a direct construction cost.

Sales and Marketing Expenses

Review the results of your marketing activities during the past year. Using your answers to the questions in Section Three, you should be now able to develop a marketing plan that targets the activities you plan to pursue next year.

Following are the major categories within the sales and marketing expenses section of the financial spreadsheet. Refer to the NAHB Chart of Accounts for a more detailed description of the individual accounts in each category.

Sales Salaries and Commissions: Include compensation including base salary and commissions paid to sales personnel.

Payroll Taxes and Benefits: Include the payroll taxes and benefits relating to sales personnel. You may want to track the payroll taxes and benefits relating to sales personnel within the general and administrative section of the spreadsheet. For payroll taxes, budget for the time when your people go over the tax limits (e.g., federal unemployment taxes are only paid on the first $8,000 of wages. Once the individual reaches $8,000 of wages, unemployment taxes are no longer calculated).

Sales Office Expenses: For builders with a separate sales office, include the operating costs of the office in this category.

Advertising and Sales Promotion: Try to identify the month during which you expect to incur a given cost. For example, if you plan to participate in a parade of homes, budget for the registration fee in the month it is due and the out-of-pocket costs for the parade when you expect to pay them.

Model Home Maintenance: Include all costs of maintaining your model homes. If your office is in your model, you may want to include the operating expenses within the general and administrative category.

Sales and Marketing Fees: Include items such as market research and other fees.

Depreciation: Include depreciation on items such as model home furnishings and other sales and marketing department assets. You may want to include all of your depreciation expenses within the general and administrative category.

Other Marketing Expenses: Include any other sales and marketing expenses not otherwise classified, including sales concessions.

General and Administrative Expenses

Following are the major categories within the general and administrative expenses section of the financial spreadsheet. Refer to the NAHB Chart of Accounts for a more detailed description of the individual accounts in each category.

Salaries and Wages: Include the salaries and wages of administrative personnel. Identify the gross wages and related taxes in the actual month that it will be made (e.g., for weekly payrolls, you will have some months with four weeks and some with five weeks).

Payroll Taxes and Benefits: Include the payroll taxes and benefits relating to thc owncr and administrative personnel whose salaries are included within the general and administrative expense section of the operating budget. If you are not using the payroll taxes and benefits sections within the sales and marketing and indirect cost sections of the spreadsheet, include the payroll taxes and benefits relating to all employees whose salaries and wages are included within the operating budget. For payroll taxes, budget for the time when your people go over the tax limits (e.g., federal unemployment taxes are only paid on the first $8,000 of wages. Once the individual reaches $8,000 of wages, unemployment taxes are no longer calculated).

Office Expenses: Include all expenses relating to operating the company's offices. Review all of your leases for office space and equipment; are there any anticipated increases scheduled for the upcoming year? Examine your communications charges for the last several months. Challenge your fixed monthly charges on your office phone bill (you may be paying for lines you don't have or don't need). Cellular charges are often difficult to keep under control. Analyze your calling patterns and look into going onto a calling plan that best matches your usage. Challenge your employees' cell phone use–are they constantly on the phone to cover up for lack of planning on the job?

Computer Expenses: Include all computer-related expenses except for hardware and software purchases that should be capitalized. Computer hardware purchases as well as large-dollar software purchases should be capitalized and reported on the balance sheet input worksheet.

Vehicle, Travel, and Entertainment: Include all costs relating to operating administrative vehicles as well as company travel and entertainment expenses. It's generally hard to budget for repairs and maintenance on a monthly basis since you can't predict when your vehicles will break down. Planning for scheduled maintenance on your vehicle is one way of smoothing out the guesswork. In the long run, routine maintenance usually leads to longer vehicle life and less unplanned expenditures.

Taxes: Include all anticipated taxes (except corporate income taxes) due during the year for which you are developing your operating budget. Real estate taxes relating to homes to be built should be included as a direct construction cost.

Insurance: Include fire and extended coverage on buildings and contents, property damage and liability on vehicles, and costs of liability insurance other than vehicles, including general and product liability insurance. Do not include worker's compensation insurance (which should be included in the payroll taxes and benefits section) or builder's risk insurance (which should be included in indirect construction costs).

Professional Services: Include professional fees paid for legal, accounting, and consulting services, as well as recruiting and hiring fees. Legal fees incurred in connection with land purchases should be included as part of your land costs, while legal fees relating to house closings should be included as a direct construction cost.

Depreciation: Include depreciation on company buildings, administrative vehicles, furniture and fixtures, computers, office machines, and other equipment.

General and Administrative Expenses, Other: Include any other general and administrative expenses not otherwise classified.

Income Statement

The income statement is a summary of a business entity's revenue, expenses, and net income (earnings) or loss for a specific period of time– a month, quarter, or a year. Net income or loss for the period becomes part of the balance sheet by increasing (net income) or decreasing (net loss) the owner's capital.

The upper part of the income statement should show the overall amount of revenue and costs relating to earnings from construction activities. The lower portion of the income statement reflects expenses incurred in the operation of the business. These include a summary of the expenses from your operating budget.

Most of the information on the pro forma income statement flows from other worksheets. Following is a discussion of the information that flows into the income statement from other parts of the financial spreadsheet.

Revenue: This number is computed from information entered on the sales/starts/closings worksheet. The number of units closed for the year for each community/type is multiplied by the related average sales price to determine the annual revenue.

Direct Construction Costs: This number is computed from information entered on the sales/starts/closings worksheet. The number of units closed for the year for each community/type is multiplied by the related average construction costs per home to determine the annual direct construction costs.

Land Costs: This number is computed from information entered on the sales/starts/closings worksheet. The number of units closed for the year for each community/type is multiplied by the related average land costs per home to determine the annual direct construction costs.

Operating Expenses: Each of the line items in this section is pulled from the operating expenses worksheet (category total column).

Other Income: Enter the amount of net earnings from other activities not related to your construction operations projected for the year. Include in this category items such as interest and dividend income, earnings from joint ventures and partnerships, and land profit.

Owner's Compensation: This figure is pulled from the category total of the owner's compensation line (account 8010) in the operating expense worksheet.

Balance Sheet

The balance sheet shows a business entity's assets, liabilities, and equity at a specific date. Assets are items owned by the business; liabilities include items the business owes. Equity is the owners' interest in the enterprise. Among other items, the balance sheet shows how much cash a builder has in the bank, how much money is owed to him, what he owes, the cost of in-progress houses, and what the business is worth at a given point in time.

The following information flows into the pro forma balance sheet from other worksheets in the financial spreadsheet. Refer to the NAHB Chart of Accounts in the appendix for definitions of the accounts on the balance sheet worksheet.

Cash: The cash balance as of the end of the pro forma period is pulled from the cash flow worksheet. It's found in the cell containing the ending cash balance as of the end of the pro forma period.

Fixed Assets: On the bottom of the balance sheet worksheet you can enter the amount of fixed asset additions and deletions planned for during the year. Balance sheet balances are computed by adding the additions and subtracting the deletions from the previous year's balance sheet.

Capital Stock: The amount in this line is pulled from the previous year's balance sheet. If you anticipate issuing additional stock during the year, you should update this number.

Retained Earnings: This amount is computed by adding the previous year's retained earnings to the previous year's net income and subtracting the previous year's owner's draws and distributions.

Net Income: This amount is pulled from the income statement worksheet.

Here are some tips for budgeting for the other lines within your pro forma balance sheet:

Accounts and Notes Receivable: Review your anticipated work in progress as of the end of the reporting period and project the amount of customer billings to be prepared (and that will not be collected) during the last month of your pro forma period. Also include anticipated payments due within one year on notes and mortgages receivable.

Direct Construction Costs: Review your anticipated work in progress as of the end of the reporting period to project the costs incurred on homes in progress. From your sales/starts/closings worksheet, first determine the number of starts you don't anticipate closing by the end of your reporting period. Use your average days under construction to anticipate each in-progress home's construction stage, and determine a percentage of anticipated total construction costs. Multiply the anticipated percentage completion by the average construction cost to compute the projected cost of the homes in progress.

Finished Units and Other Inventories: Project the number of homes you anticipate completing but not closing as of the end of the pro forma reporting period.

Construction Loans Payable: This number should be tied to borrowings on your inventory as of the end of the pro forma reporting period. Multiply the anticipated percentage of completion by the average construction loan commitment to compute the projected construction loan outstanding. Also add any loans anticipated on finished units and land development.

Contract Deposits: Using figures from the sales/starts/closings worksheet, multiply the average customer deposit per home by the number of sold but unclosed homes anticipated at the end of the reporting period.

After you've done a first draft of your operating budget, sit back and examine the overall numbers. Add your targeted net profit to your operating expenses to determine the amount of gross profit you need for the year. Once you know the dollars of gross profit needed, you can determine the markup you need to reach your goals.

For example, suppose you expect to produce five houses this year with an average sales price of $300,000 for total anticipated sales of $1,500,000. If you want to achieve a 10 percent net return, your targeted net income is $150,000. If your overhead for the year totaled $300,000, you will need $450,000 of gross profit (sales less direct construction costs–all costs not accounted for in your operating budget) to hit your goal.

To determine the markup you need, first compute your targeted cost of sales by subtracting your targeted gross profit ($450,000) from your anticipated sales ($1,500,000). In this example, cost of sales would be $1,050,000. To determine your markup, divide sales by cost of sales ($1,500,000/$1,050,000), which totals a markup of 1.42.

If you find the markup you must achieve to meet your goals is unreasonably high, it's time to go back and challenge your operating expenses. Have you built in capacity to be able to handle more volume? Will the market give you the opportunity to sell more than the five homes in your original plan? Make the necessary changes in your budget so you can realistically meet your net income goal.

Cash Flow

All builders should engage in long- and short-term cash flow planning. It's a key component of financial success. Long-term cash flow planning should be an integral part of the budgeting process. Do it by examining your cash sources and requirements on a monthly basis. In addition to developing a monthly cash flow forecast, we suggest that you begin to look at weekly cash inflows and outflows. We recommend using a six- to eight-week rolling schedule.

After you have identified your monthly operating expenses in the month you anticipate them occurring, adjust your total expenses for other cash flow items. Deduct items such as depreciation since it's a non-cash expense and add in non-expense related cash items such as note payments (the interest portion should be considered as an expense, while the principal payments affect cash flow), cash payments of other liabilities, cash purchases for equipment, and cash payments for federal and state income taxes. After completing this process you should have identified the amount of cash you need monthly to operate your company.

The next step in annual cash forecasting is to look at cash flow from jobs. Depending on the number of units you build, you can prepare this budget by unit or by subdivision. You need to consult four items while developing your job cash flow: your draw schedule (whether from the bank or from your customer), construction schedule, payment terms for your trade contractors and suppliers, and job estimate. With these items in hand, you should easily be able to predict cash inflows and outflows for your jobs.

When you combine your cash flow from jobs with the cash outflows anticipated

from operations, you will be able to identify the months in which you will have excess cash and those in which you'll have cash shortfalls. Use this projection to make strategic decisions for the year. For example, do you need to develop a line of credit to smooth out your cash flow? Should you start a spec home to provide cash flow from your construction loan? Do you need to renegotiate payment terms on a note coming due?

The cash flow worksheet will help you develop your monthly cash flow projection. Here is a discussion of the items that flow from other worksheets.

Deposits: This number is computed from the sales/starts/closings worksheet by multiplying the average customer deposit per home by the number of homes sold each month.

Closings: This number is computed from the sales/starts/closings worksheet by multiplying the average sales price per home by the number of homes closed and subtracting the number of homes closed multiplied by the average customer deposit per home.

Indirect Costs: This number is pulled from the operating expense worksheet from the total indirect costs line minus total indirect depreciation expense.

Financing Expenses: This number is pulled from the operating expense worksheet from the total finance expense line.

Sales and Marketing Expenses: This number is pulled from the operating expense worksheet from the total sales and marketing expense.

General and Administrative Expenses: This number is pulled from the operating expense worksheet from the total general and administrative expense costs line minus total general and administration depreciation expense.

Ratio Analysis

Ratio analysis is a mathematical technique for assessing a company's current financial posture using information from the income statement and balance sheet.

The keys to ratio analysis involve setting goals like those discussed within each of the definitions above, and monitoring how well you meet them. During your planning process you should also develop goals for the ratios discussed below.

Following are several main ratios that should be reviewed at least quarterly. These ratios are computed on the balance sheet worksheet. Compare your projected financial ratios with industry norms as defined below. Justify any significant deviations.

Current ratio: This is the most popular measure of a company's solvency. A solvent company can meet its current debts with current assets and can provide for growth without borrowing.

The current ratio is calculated by dividing current assets by current liabilities. Current assets are those assets that are easily liquidated during the normal course of one year of operations, and include items such as cash, accounts receivable, and work in progress. Current liabilities include all debts due upon demand, such as accounts payable, billings in excess of costs (over-billings under the percentage of completion method of accounting), and debt secured by work in progress as well the portions of long-term notes payable within the accounting year.

The higher the ratio, the more capable the company is of meeting its current obligations. A ratio of 1 to 3, meaning the firm has $1.30 of current assets for every dollar of current liability, is often considered the ideal. A ratio below 1 to 0 or a downward trend from 1 to 3 can indicate potential cash flow problems. A current ratio above 1 to 6 can indicate reluctance to fully use your credit position.

Debt-to-equity ratio: This measures the extent to which borrowed funds are used for the business operation. It is commonly referred to as the company's leverage factor. The ratio is calculated by dividing total liabilities by total equity (net worth). The higher the ratio, the more risk creditors assume.

Builders with a high debt-to-equity ratio may have trouble getting construction loans. If they get the loans, they'll probably pay higher rates than builders who are not so highly leveraged. Conversely, a lower ratio usually indicates that the company has more borrowing capacity and greater long-term financial stability. A debt-to-equity ratio of less than 4 to 1 is considered good.

Inventory turnover ratio: This measures the movement of inventory during a given accounting period. It allows a builder to intelligently evaluate inventory levels. This ratio measures the amount of sales to total inventory.

The most accurate way to measure inventory turnover is to add the beginning inventory and ending inventory for the year and then divide that sum by two. This gives you an average inventory for the year. It is important to use the average inventory because lower or higher amounts of inventory at one time or another may result in an inaccurate picture of inventory turnover. Production builders should strive for turnover ratios of 2 to 4 times per year. The faster you can complete and settle your homes while maintaining the quality level your customers expect, the better.

Return on equity: Often called the profit-to-net-worth ratio, "earning power," or return on investment (ROI), return on equity is perhaps the most significant measure of profitability from the owner's point of view. It measures the rate of return on the investment in the business. This percentage ratio is calculated by dividing net income before tax (from the income statement) by the total net worth (from the balance sheet). An unusually high ratio (something approaching 100 percent) may indicate too little investment in the company, while a low percentage usually indicates poor performance, which may result from unprofitable operations or inappropriate use of investment dollars to generate sales volume.

Equity is the investment you made in your building company. It consists of your initial investment plus profits kept in the business. If you decided to put that equity in the bank, you might get a return on your investment of 3 percent. If you put it into the stock market, you may lose it. If you'd hit the right dot-com before the tech companies tanked, that equity might have earned a return of more than 100 percent. Your company's ROI tells you the return you made by keeping your investment in your building company as compared to other possible investments.

APPENDIX

RECOMMENDED READINGS

The following books offer additional information on business planning and business management practices:

The Great Game of Business, Jack Stack.
The Millionaire Next Door, Thomas J. Stanley and William D. Danko.
Leadership, Rudolph W. Giuliani and Ken Kurson.
Management Mistakes & Successes, Robert F. Hartley.
Hiring the Best: A Manager's Guide to Effective Interviewing, Martin Yate.
Harvard Business Review on Leadership, Harvard Business School Press.
Harvard Business Review on Change, Harvard Business School Press.
The 7 Habits of Highly Effective People, Stephen R. Covey.
The E-Myth Contractor: Why Most Contractors' Businesses Don't Work and What To Do About It, Michael E. Gerber.
The E-Myth Revisited: Why Most Small Businesses Don't Work and What To Do About It, Michael E. Gerber.
The Winner Within: A Life Plan for Team Players, Pat Riley.
The Discipline of Market Leaders: Choose Your Customers, Narrow Your Focus, Dominate Your Market, Michael Treacy and Fred Wiersema.
Good to Great: Why Some Companies Make the Leap . . . and Others Don't, Jim Collins.
The One Minute Manager, Kenneth H. Blanchard and Spencer Johnson.
Who Moved My Cheese? An Amazing Way to Deal With Change In Your Work and In Your Life, Kenneth H. Blanchard and Spencer Johnson.

NAHB CHART OF ACCOUNTS

Part A. Outline of NAHB Chart of Accounts

1000–1990	**Assets**
1000–1090	**Cash**
1010	Petty cash
1020	Cash on deposit, general
1030	Cash on deposit, payroll
1040	Cash on deposit, savings and money market
1050	Cash on deposit, held in escrow
1100–1190	**Short-Term Investments**
1110	Certificates of deposit
1120	Marketable securities
1130	Government securities
1190	Other short-term Investments
1200–1290	**Receivables**
1210	Accounts receivable, trade
1220	Accounts receivable, other
1230	Notes receivable
1250	Mortgage notes receivable, current year
1260	Due on construction and development loans
1270	Accrued interest receivable
1280	Allowance for doubtful accounts
1290	Retentions (retainage) receivable
1300–1390	**Inventories**
1310	Construction materials inventory
1320	Land held for development
1330	Property held for remodeling
1400–1490	**Construction Work in Progress**

1410	Land and land development
1412	Accumulated allocations, land and land development costs
1420	Developed lots
1430	Direct construction cost
1440	Indirect construction cost
1470	Cost in excess of billings
1500–1590	**Finished Units and Other Inventory**
1510	Finished units
1520	Model homes
1530	Trade-ins and repossessions
1600–1690	**Other Current Assets**
1610	Refundable deposits
1620	Prepaid expenses
1630	Employee advances
1650	Due from affiliated companies or subsidiaries
1660	Due from officers, stockholders, owners or partners
1670	Deposits on plans
1690	Other current assets
1700–1790	**Investments and Other Assets**
1710	Investments, long-term
1720	Cash surrender value of officers' life insurance
1730	Investments in affiliated entities
1750	Mortgage notes receivable, long-term
1760	Due from affiliated companies or subsidiaries, long-term
1770	Due from officers, owners, stockholders, long-term
1780	Organization cost
1800–1890	**Property, Plant, and Equipment**
1810	Land
1820	Buildings
1825	Rental property
1827	Recreation amenities
1830	Office furniture and equipment
1840	Vehicles
1850	Construction equipment
1870	Model home furnishings
1880	Leasehold improvements
1890	Computer equipment and software
1900–1990	**Accumulated Depreciation**

1920 Accumulated depreciation, buildings
1925 Accumulated depreciation, rental properties
1927 Accumulated depreciation, recreation amenities
1930 Accumulated depreciation, office furniture and equipment
1940 Accumulated depreciation, vehicles
1950 Accumulated depreciation, construction equipment
1970 Accumulated depreciation, model home furnishings
1980 Accumulated depreciation, leasehold improvements
1990 Accumulated depreciation, computer equipment and software

2000–2090 Deposits by Customers
2010 Contract deposits
2030 Tenant security deposit
2040 Advance rent collected
2100–2190 Accounts Payable
2110 Accounts payable, trade
2120 Retentions payable
2190 Accounts payable, other
2200–2290 Notes Payable
2200 Line of credit payable
2220 Acquisitions and development loans payable (old 252 in prior accounts)
2230 Construction loans payable
2240 Current portion of long-term debt
2290 Notes payable, other
2300–2490 Other Current Liabilities
2310 Social Security and Medicare
2320 Federal payroll tax withheld and accrued
2330 State payroll tax withheld and accrued
2340 Other payroll withholdings
2345 Union withholding and benefits payable
2350 Sales and use taxes payable
2360 Real estate taxes payable
2370 Income taxes payable
2390 Accrued interest payable
2400 Accrued salaries and wages payable
2410 Accrued commissions payable
2411 Accrued pension and profit-sharing expenses

2420	Workers' compensation insurance payable
2425	Other accrued expenses
2430	Deferred income
2440	Due to affiliated companies or subsidiaries
2450	Due to officers, stockholders, owners, and partners
2480	Billings in excess of costs
2490	Other current liabilities
2500–2890	**Long-Term Liabilities**
2510	Long-term notes payable
2530	Mortgage notes payable
2600	Deferred income tax payable
2610	Due to affiliated companies or subsidiaries, long-term
2620	Due to officers, stockholders, owners, long-term, and partners
2700	Other long-term liabilities
2900–2990	**Owners' Equity**
2900	Common stock
2910	Additional paid in capital
2920	Retained earnings
2930	Treasury stock
2940	Unrealized holding gain
2950	Partnership or proprietorship account
2960	Distributions, dividends, and draws

3000–3990	**Sales, Revenues, and Cost of Sales**
3000–3490	**Sales and Revenues**
3000	Sales, land held for development
3050	Sales, developed lots
3100	Sales, single-family speculative
3110	Sales, single-family production
3120	Sales, single-family custom designed
3125	Sales, single-family custom, no land
3130	Sales, residential remodeling
3133	Sales, commercial and industrial remodeling
3135	Sales, insurance restoration
3137	Sales, repairs
3140	Sales, multifamily
3150	Sales, commercial and industrial

3160	Sales, trade-ins, and repossessions
3190	Sales, other
3200	Rental property income
3210	Common area reimbursements
3220	Other reimbursements
3230	Parking fee income
3240	Amenities and facilities income
3360	Construction management fee income
3370	Design fees collected
3400	Miscellaneous income
3410	Interest income
3420	Dividend income
3450	Earned discounts
3490	Sales concessions and discounts
3500–3790	**Cost of Sales**
3500	Cost of sales, land held for development
3550	Cost of sales, developed lots
3600	Cost of sales, single-family speculative
3610	Cost of sales, single-family production
3620	Cost of sales, single-family custom designed
3625	Cost of sales, single-family custom, no land
3630	Cost of sales, remodeling
3633	Cost of sales, commercial and industrial remodeling
3635	Cost of sales, insurance restoration
3637	Cost of sales, repairs
3640	Cost of sales, multifamily
3650	Cost of sales, commercial and industrial
3660	Cost of sales, trade-ins
3690	Cost of sales, other
3700	Direct construction cost for prior periods
3800–3899	**Costs of Construction–Remodeling**
3810	Direct labor
3820	Labor burden
3830	Building material
3840	Subcontractors
3850	Rental equipment
3860	Other direct construction costs
3870	Professional design fees

4000–4990	**Indirect Construction Cost**
4000–4090	**Salaries and Wages**
4010	Superintendents
4020	Laborers
4030	Production manager
4040	Architects, drafters, estimators, and purchasers
4050	Other indirect construction wages
4100–4190	**Payroll Taxes and Benefits**
4110	Payroll taxes
4120	Workers' compensation insurance
4130	Health and accident insurance
4140	Retirement, pension, and profit sharing
4150	Union benefits
4190	Other benefits
4200–4290	**Field Office Expenses**
4210	Rent, field office
4230	Repairs and maintenance, field office
4250	Utilities, field office
4260	Telephone, field office
4265	Mobile phones, pagers, and radios
4290	Other field office expenses
4300–4390	**Field Warehouse and Storage Expenses**
4310	Rent, field warehouse and storage
4330	Repairs and maintenance, field warehouse and storage
4350	Utilities, field warehouse and storage
4360	Telephone, field warehouse and storage
4400–4490	**Construction Vehicles, Travel, and Entertainment**
4410	Lease payments, construction vehicles
4420	Mileage reimbursement
4430	Repairs and maintenance, construction vehicles
4440	Operating expenses, construction vehicles
4450	Taxes, licenses, and insurance, construction vehicles
4460	Travel, construction department
4470	Customer business entertainment, construction
4480	Training and education, construction
4490	Recruiting fees and expenses, construction
4500–4590	**Construction Equipment**
4510	Rent, construction equipment

4530	Repairs and maintenance, construction equipment
4540	Operating expenses, construction equipment
4550	Taxes and insurance, construction equipment
4560	Small tools and supplies
4600–4690	**Expenses for Maintaining Unsold Units and Units Under Construction**
4610	Temporary utilities
4620	Trash maintenance
4640	Lawn care
4650	Utilities, completed units
4660	Repairs and maintenance, completed units
4700–4790	**Warranty and Customer Service**
4710	Salaries and wages, warranty
4720	Material, warranty
4730	Subcontractor, warranty
4790	Other, warranty expenses
4800–4890	**Depreciation Expenses**
4820	Depreciation, construction office
4830	Depreciation, warehouse
4840	Depreciation, construction vehicles
4850	Depreciation, construction equipment
4900–4990	**Other**
4910	Insurance and bonding expenses
4920	Builders risk insurance
4990	Absorbed indirect costs

5000–5990 Financing Expenses

5000–5090	**Interest**
5010	Interest on line of credit
5020	Interest on notes payable
5030	Interest expense on developed lots
5040	Interest incurred on construction loans
5050	Interest on completed inventory
5090	Interest expense, other
5100–5190	**Construction Loan Points and Fees**
5120	Points and fees
5130	Appraisal and related fees
5140	Inspection fees

5200–5290	**Closing Costs**
5210	Closing costs
5220	Title and recording
5230	Fees, commitment
6000–6990	**Sales and Marketing Expenses**
6000–6090	**Sales Salaries, and Commissions**
6010	Sales manager's compensation
6030	Salaries, sales personnel
6040	Sales commissions, in-house
6050	Sales commissions, outside
6090	Other sales office salaries and wages
6100–6190	**Payroll Taxes and Benefits, Sales and Marketing**
6110	Payroll taxes, sales and marketing
6120	Workers' compensation insurance, sales and marketing
6130	Health and accident insurance, sales and marketing
6140	Retirement, pension, and profit-sharing plans, sales and marketing
6190	Other benefits
6200–6290	**Sales Office Expenses**
6210	Rent, sales office
6230	Repairs and maintenance, sales office
6250	Utilities, sales office
6260	Telephone, sales office
6270	Supplies, sales office
6300–6390	**Advertising and Sales Promotion**
6310	Print advertising
6320	Radio advertising
6325	Television advertising
6330	Internet fees, web page design and maintenance costs
6340	Brochures and catalogues
6350	Signs
6355	Billboards
6365	Promotions
6370	Agency commissions
6380	Multiple listing fees
6390	Public relations
6395	Referral Fees
6400–6490	**Sales Vehicles, Travel, and Entertainment**

6410 Lease payments, sales vehicles
6420 Mileage reimbursement
6430 Repairs and maintenance, sales vehicles
6440 Operating expenses, sales vehicles
6450 Taxes, licenses, insurance, sales vehicles
6460 Travel, sales and marketing
6470 Customer business entertainment
6600–6690 Model Home Maintenance
6610 Rent or lease payments, model home furnishings
6620 Model home rent or lease payments
6625 Model home decorating fees
6630 Repairs and maintenance, model homes
6650 Utilities, model homes
6670 Lawn and landscaping care model homes
6680 Cleanup, model homes
6690 Interest on model homes
6700–6790 Sales and Marketing Fees
6710 Market research and consultation
6720 Interior design fee
6770 Recruiting fees and expenses, sales and marketing personnel
6780 Training and education expenses
6800–6890 Depreciation
6810 Depreciation, sales office
6830 Depreciation, sales vehicles
6870 Depreciation, model home furnishings, and decorations
6900–6990 Other Marketing Expenses
6930 Sales concessions
6940 Buydowns
6999 Other sales and marketing expenses

7000–7990 Operating and Management Expenses, Rental Operations

7000–7090 Property Management
7010 Property manager's compensation
7030 Salaries and wages, property management personnel
7040 Commissions, in-house
7050 Commissions, outside
7060 Salaries and wages to maintenance personnel

7070	Payroll taxes and benefits, rental operations
7072	Workers' compensation insurance, rental
7073	Health and accident insurance, rental
7074	Retirement, pension, and profit-sharing plans, rental
7079	Other benefits, rental
7100–7190	**Rental Expenses**
7110	Advertising
7130	Credit reports
7190	Other rental expenses
7200–7290	**Administrative Expenses, Rental Operations**
7220	Management and service fees
7230	Office expenses
7240	Telephone
7250	Tenant bad debts
7260	Collection costs
7290	Other administrative expenses
7300–7390	**Professional Services, Rental Operations**
7310	Legal services
7320	Accounting services
7330	Market research
7390	Other professional services, rental operations
7400–7490	**Operating Expenses, Rental Operations**
7410	Utilities
7420	Engineering
7430	Janitorial
7440	Trash removal service
7450	Exterminating
7460	Snow removal
7470	Other contractual services
7480	Vehicles and equipment, rental operations
7490	Other rental operations expenses
7500–7590	**Taxes and Insurance, Rental Operations**
7510	Real estate property taxes
7520	Personal property taxes
7530	Franchise taxes
7540	License fees
7560	Workers' compensation insurance
7570	Insurance, rental operations
7590	Other taxes and insurance, rental operations

7600–7690	**Maintenance and Repairs, Rental Operations**
7610	Tenant redecorating
7630	Maintenance contracts and services
7640	Ground maintenance and repairs
7650	Vehicle maintenance and repairs, rental operations
7660	Equipment maintenance and repairs, rental operations
7670	Amenities maintenance and repairs
7700–7790	**Financing Expense, Rental Operations**
7710	Interest on mortgage payable
7720	Interest on long-term notes payable
7800–7890	**Depreciation Expenses, Rental Operations**
7810	Depreciation, building
7820	Depreciation, maintenance equipment
7830	Depreciation, vehicles
7840	Depreciation, furniture and fixtures
7850	Depreciation, amenities
7890	Other depreciation
7900–7990	**Other Management and Operating Expenses**

8000–8990	**General and Administrative Expenses**
8000–8090	**Salaries and Wages**
8010	Salaries, owners
8020	Salaries, officers
8030	Salaries, management
8050	Salaries and wages, office and clerical
8090	Other general and administrative salaries and wages
8100–8190	**Payroll Taxes and Benefits**
8110	Payroll taxes
8120	Workers' compensation insurance
8130	Health and accident insurance
8140	Retirement, pension, and profit-sharing plans
8190	Other employee benefits
8200–8290	**Office Expenses**
8210	Rent
8220	Office equipment rental
8230	Repairs and maintenance, administrative office space
8240	Repairs and maintenance, administrative office equipment
8250	Utilities, administrative office
8260	Telephone, administrative office

8270	Office supplies, administrative office
8280	Postage and deliveries
8290	Miscellaneous expenses, administrative office
8300–8390	**Computer Expenses**
8310	Computer supplies
8320	Leases, computer hardware
8330	Leases, computer software
8350	Repairs and maintenance, computer equipment
8360	Maintenance, computer software
8400–8490	**Vehicles, Travel, and Entertainment**
8410	Lease, administrative vehicles
8420	Mileage reimbursement
8430	Repairs and maintenance, administration vehicles
8440	Operating expense, administration vehicles
8450	Taxes, licenses, and insurance, administration vehicles
8460	Travel
8470	Customer business expense
8480	Meeting expenses
8490	In-house meeting expenses
8500–8590	**Taxes**
8510	Sales-and-use taxes
8520	Real estate taxes
8530	Personal property taxes
8540	License fees
8590	Other taxes
8600–8690	**Insurance**
8610	Hazard insurance/property insurance
8630	General liability insurance
8690	Other insurance
8700–8790	**Professional Services**
8710	Accounting services
8720	Legal services
8730	Consulting services
8770	Recruiting and hiring
8790	Other professional expenses
8800–8890	**Depreciation Expenses**
8810	Depreciation, buildings
8830	Depreciation, vehicles
8840	Depreciation, furniture, and equipment

8860	Amortization of leasehold improvement
8870	Depreciation computer equipment and software
8880	Amortization of organization cost
8890	Depreciation, other
8900–8990	**General and Administrative Expenses, Other**
8900	Bad debts
8910	Contributions
8911	Contributions, political
8920	Dues and subscriptions
8950	Bank charges
8960	Penalties
8990	Training and education expenses

9000–9990	**Other Income and Expenses**
9100–9190	**Other Income**
9100	Income from partnerships, joint ventures, S-Corps, and LLCs
9150	Gain or loss on sale of assets
9190	Other
9200–9290	**Other Expenses**
9200	**Extraordinary Expenses**
9300–9390	**Provision for Income Taxes**
9300	Provision for federal income taxes
9320	Provision for state income taxes
9330	Provision for local income taxes

Part B. The Complete NAHB Chart of Accounts

1000–1990	**Assets**
1000–1090	**Cash**
1010	**Petty Cash**–All of a company's petty cash accounts, whether maintained in office or by construction superintendent in the field.
1020	**Cash on Deposit, General**–Demand deposits in bank for all regular trade receipts and disbursements.
1030	**Cash on Deposit, Payroll**–Demand deposits in bank for payroll disbursements only. Generally, companies that employ their own crews and write a large number of payroll checks maintain a separate checking account to

cover payroll. For each pay period, a check for the total amount of the payroll is written against the general account and deposited in the payroll account.

1040 **Cash on Deposit, Savings and Money Market**–Deposits in savings and money market accounts.

1050 **Cash on Deposit, Held in Escrow**–Cash held at title companies, disbursing agents, and financial institutions representing refundable customer deposits, completion escrows, or other escrowed funds.

1100–1190 Short-Term Investments

1110 **Certificates of Deposit**–Funds deposited in interest-bearing certificates of deposit (CDs) maturing in less than 1 year.

1120 **Marketable Securities**–Funds invested in readily marketable stock of unaffiliated companies that management intends to dispose of within 1 year. In accordance with generally accepted accounting principles (GAAP), these investments should be carried at the lower of aggregate cost or market value. To adjust, credit this account and debit 2940 (Unrealized Holding Loss).

1130 **Government Securities**–Funds invested in securities issued by federal, state, or local authorities maturing in less than 1 year.

1190 **Other Short-Term Investments**–Funds invested in other instruments for set periods (usually less than 1 year) that earn interest or dividend income.

1200–1290 Receivables

1210 **Accounts Receivable, Trade**–Amounts due to the business for construction, including customers' orders for extras, management services, or other services performed on open account.

1220 **Accounts Receivable, Other**–Amounts due to the business for services not otherwise classified.

1230 **Notes Receivable**–Unpaid balance due to the company on notes received in full or partial settlement of open or short-term accounts.

1250 **Mortgage Notes Receivable, Current Year**–Mortgages taken from purchasers in lieu of cash. Payments due within 12 months.

1260 **Due on Construction and Development Loans**–Amounts due from financial institutions on construction and development loans. The balance on this account represents the amount of cash available from construction and development loans. When a loan is approved, debit this account to show how much cash is available through the loan and credit account 2220 (Acquisitions, Development, and Construction Loans Payable). As you draw cash from the loan, you decrease or credit Account 1260 (Due on construction and development loans) to show how much cash is left to draw from the loan. As an alternative, you can record draws against construction loans directly to account 2220 (Acquisitions, Development, and Construction Loans Payable).

1265 **Costs in Excess of Billings**–This account is used mostly by remodelers, custom builders, and commercial builders to record costs that exceed their estimated costs (sometimes referred to as under billing) based on the percentage of completion method.

1270 **Accrued Interest Receivable**–Interest earned but not received from all sources such as bonds, notes, and mortgages.

1280 **Allowance for Doubtful Accounts**–A contra account that has a credit balance reflecting the potential uncollectible amounts of any account in the receivables classification. A contra account serves the purpose of reducing the balance of an account (in this case, accounts receivable) without changing the account itself.

1290 **Retentions (Retainage) Receivable**–Amounts withheld by customers on progress billings. When retentions become due, Account 1210 (Accounts receivable trade) is credited while Account 2210 (Accounts payable, trade) is debited.

1300–1390 Inventories

1310 **Construction Materials Inventory**–Control account for book value of construction materials purchased and stored rather than delivered directly to a job in progress. As materials are allocated to a specific job, the cost is transferred and debited to Account 1430 (Direct construction cost) and credited to Account 1310 (Construction materials inventory). Excess materials purchased directly for a specific job and originally debited to Account 1430 should be debited to Account 1310 and credited to Account 1430, if the materials are transferred to inventory; or they should be allocated to the cost of the house for which the materials are used.

1320 **Land Held for Development**–Control account for cost of land purchased for future development. The cost of land increases by recording fees, legal fees, and other acquisition costs. Debit cost of land to Account 1410 (Land and land development) at time land is to be developed, and credit Account 1320 (Land held for development).

1330 **Property Held for Remodeling**–Acquisition costs for properties held for future improvement or remodeling. Once the work is completed, they may be sold or held for investment.

1400–1490 Work in Progress

1410 **Land and Land Development**–Control account for all land and land development costs (see part F.) Cumulative cost of land and land development, including cost of raw land, financing and interest, land planning, engineering, grading, streets, curb and gutters, sidewalks, storm sewers, temporary utilities, professional fees, permits and other costs pertaining to the development of the raw land.

1412 **Accumulated Allocations, Land, and Land Development Costs**–Accumulated write-offs to cost of sales for land and land development costs. At the time of closing, debit the cost of the lot to the appropriate cost of sales account in the 3500 to 3700 series.

1420 **Developed Lots**–Cost of lots developed prior to purchase to be used for construction. When a house is closed, debit the cost to the appropriate cost of sales account in the 3500 to 3700 series.

1430 **Direct Construction Cost**–Control account for all direct construction costs (see Part D), including permits, direct labor, materials, subcontractors, equipment rentals, and any other direct charge to the units under construction. This account must be supported by job cost subsidiaries that detail the cost of each construction unit. Also included are finance and interest charges during construction. Never include in this account marketing costs or indirect construction costs. When a house is closed, debit the cost to the appropriate cost of sales account in the 3500 to 3700 series.

1440 **Indirect Construction Cost**–A control account that requires a detailed breakdown in a subsidiary ledger of the different elements of cost. By adding an additional two digits to establish sub accounts, a detailed breakdown of the indirect construction costs can be accommodated in the general chart of accounts (see Part E). Indirect construction costs are necessary costs of building that cannot be directly, easily, or economically attributed to a specific house or job. These costs are classified as assets–part of the value of inventories–since they contribute to the value of the work in progress. The Internal Revenue Service and GAAP (Generally Accepted Accounting Procedures) generally require that real estate and construction inventories include the proportional share of indirect costs. When a house is closed, debit the proportional share of the cost in the 3500 to 3700 series. An alternative method of treating indirect costs is to record the cost within the 4000 Series an operating expense classification. In order to comply with IRS and GAAP requirements when using the alternative method, allocate the proportional share of indirect construction costs to work in process inventories.

1500–1590 Finished Units and Other Inventory

1510 **Finished Units**–Accumulated direct and indirect construction costs of units completed but not sold. Transfer from and credit Accounts 1430 (Direct construction cost) and 1440 (Indirect construction cost) at the time of completion. The cost of the lot, accumulated in Account 1420 (Developed lots), is transferred to the 3500–3700 Series at the time the sale is closed.

1520 **Model Homes**–Cost includes lot cost and direct and indirect construction costs used as models. Upon completion of model, transfer and debit costs to this account from Accounts 1420 (Developed lots), 1430 (Direct construction cost), and 1440 (Indirect construction cost), which are credited. Upon sale of model, transfer and debit costs to the 3500–3700 Series.

1530 **Trade-Ins and Repossessions**–The cost of any trade-ins acquired during a sales transaction and that are held for resale but not held as investment (including refurbishing until sold). Transfer cost to Account 3660 (Cost of sales, trade ins) when you sell the units.

1600–1690 Other Current Assets

1610 **Refundable Deposits**–Deposits paid to and held by municipalities, utilities, and other businesses for performance or completion of operation. Also include refundable plan deposits.

1620 **Prepaid Expenses**–Unexpired portions of expenses applicable to future periods for items such as insurance, rent, commitment fees, interest, and taxes. Detailed accounts for prepayments may be provided by using an additional subledger or a two-digit subclass to the main account number.

1630 **Employee Advances**–Debit for a salary advance and credit when advance is deducted from payroll or repaid by employee.

1650 **Due from Affiliates or Subsidiaries**–Short-term receivables due from affiliates or subsidiary companies.

1660 **Due from Officers, Stockholders, Owners or Partners**–Amounts currently due from officers, stockholders, owners, or partners of the business.

1690 **Other Current Assets**–Miscellaneous current assets not otherwise classified.

1700–1790 Investments and Other Assets

1710 **Investments, Long-Term**–Stocks, bonds, and other securities to be held as long- term investments. By using an additional subledger or two-digit subclass, each type of investment can be maintained in a separate account.

1720 **Cash Surrender Value of Officers' Life Insurance**–Accumulated net cash surrender value net of any outstanding loans on life insurance carried on officers of the business.

1730 **Investments in Affiliated Entities**–Capital stock of affiliated companies, subsidiaries, partnerships and joint ventures. Your company's portion of the equity or loss generated by the affiliated entity should be debited (income) or credited (loss) to this account on a period basis with the offsetting entry debited or credited to Account 9100 (Income from partnerships, joint ventures, S-Corps, and LLCs), provided that the investing company can exercise significant influence (usually more than 20 percent of the voting power) over the operations of the affiliated entity.

1750 **Mortgage Notes Receivable, Long-Term**–Amounts of mortgages that are due beyond the end of the next fiscal year end.

1760 **Due from Affiliated Companies or Subsidiaries, Long-Term**–Amounts due from affiliated companies or subsidiaries that are to be carried for a long-term period.

1770 **Due from Officers, Owners, and Stockholders, Long-Term**–Amounts due from company officers, owners, and stockholders to be carried for a long-term period. The amount may be an interest-bearing note or an open account.

1780 **Organization Cost**–Legal fees, corporate charter fees, and other organization costs that are normally capitalized. Amortization of these fees should be credited directly to this account.

1800–1890 Property, Plant, and Equipment

1810 **Land**–Cost of land acquired for the purpose of constructing company offices and warehouses and/or held for investment. Land held for future development should be included in account 1320 (Land held for development).

1820 **Buildings**–Costs relating to offices, warehouses, field offices, field warehouse, and other company structures used in the operation of the business.

1825 **Rental Property**–Cost of property owned and managed by the company held for investment. Buildings used in the operation of the business should be classified in Account 1820 (Buildings).

1827 **Recreation Amenities**–Property that the company will retain for ownership and operation. Include property to be turned over to homeowners' association in account 1430 (Direct construction cost).

1830 **Office Furniture and Equipment**–Cost of office furniture, fixtures, and small equipment used by administrative and office personnel.

1840 **Vehicles**–Cost of automobiles and trucks owned by the business.

1850 **Construction Equipment**–The cost of all construction equipment, excluding licensed motor vehicles. Charge or debit small tools of nominal value to Account 1440 (Indirect Construction Cost) or Account 4560 (Small tools and supplies).

1870 **Model Home Furnishings**–Cost of model house furniture and furnishings.

1880 **Leasehold Improvements**–Cost of improvements made to leased property.

1890 **Computer Equipment and Software**–Cost of computer hardware and software. May be segregated to improve tracking.

1900–1999 Accumulated Depreciation

1920 **Accumulated Depreciation, Buildings**–Accumulated depreciation on assets carried in Account 1820 (Buildings).

1925 **Accumulated Depreciation, Rental Properties**–Accumulated depreciation on rental properties carried in Account 1825 (Rental property).

1927 **Accumulated Depreciation, Recreation Amenities**–Accumulated depreciation on property carried in Account 1827 (Recreations amenities).

1930 **Accumulated Depreciation, Office Furniture and Equipment**–Accumulated depreciation on assets in Account 1830 (Office furniture and equipment).

1940 **Accumulated Depreciation, Vehicles**–Accumulated depreciation on assets carried in Account 1840 (Vehicles).

1950 **Accumulated Depreciation, Construction Equipment**–Accumulated depreciation on assets carried in Account 1850 (Construction equipment).

1970 **Accumulated Depreciation, Model Home Furnishings**–Accumulated depreciation on assets carried in Account1870 (Model home property furnishings).

1980 **Accumulated Depreciation, Leasehold Improvements**–Accumulated depreciation on assets in Account 1880 (Leasehold improvements).

1990 **Accumulated Depreciation, Computer Equipment and Software**–Accumulated depreciation on assets in Account 1890 (Computer equipment and software).

2000–2990 Liabilities and Owners' Equity

2000–2090 Deposits by Customers

2010 **Contract Deposits**–Down payments, earnest money, and deposits on contracts. Transfer and credit the deposit to the appropriate account in the 3000–3490 series (Sales and Revenues) when sale is closed, and debit Account 2010 (Contract deposits).

2030 **Tenant Security Deposit**–Refundable tenants' deposits held to secure proper care of unit.

2040 **Advance Rent Collected**–Rent collected from tenants that relates to a future period. When the rental income is earned, this account is debited and Account 3200 (Rental property income) is credited.

2100–2190 Accounts Payable

2110 **Accounts Payable, Trade**–Amounts payable on open account to suppliers and subcontractors.

2120 **Retentions Payable**–Amounts withheld from subcontractors until final completion and approval of their work.

2190 **Accounts Payable, Other**–Other short-term open accounts due to non-trade individuals or companies.

2200–2290 Notes Payable

2200 **Line of Credit Payable**–Outstanding balance on revolving line of credit.

2220 **Acquisition, Development, and Construction Loans Payable**–Control account for all loans from lending institutions for acquisition, development and construction financing. Detail accounts for each acquisition, development, & construction loans payable may be provided by using an additional sub-ledger or a two-digit subclass to the main account number.

2240 **Current Portion of Long-Term Debt**–Portion of principal payments included in account 2510 that are due on notes to be paid within one year.

2290 **Notes Payable, Other**–Notes payable to banks, other financial institutions, and other individuals that are due within one year.

2300–2490 Other Current Liabilities

2310 **Social Security and Medicare Withheld and Accrued**–Accumulated amounts of social security (FICA) and Medicare taxes withheld from employees payroll. This account is also used to accrue the employer's portion of these taxes.

2320 **Federal Payroll Tax Withheld**–Accumulated amounts of federal taxes withheld from employees' pay and owed to the federal government.

2330 **State and Local Payroll Tax Withheld**–Accumulated amounts of state taxes withheld from employees' pay and owed to state government. Credit funds withheld from employees' pay, and debit payments to the state income tax division. Also include disability and other state withholding taxes. For multiple states, cities, or other local government withholdings, you may want to set up a separate account or use a two-digit sub account.

2340 **Other Payroll Withholdings**–Other accumulated amounts withheld from employees' pay, such as employees' share of health insurance program. Credit funds withheld from employees' pay, and debit payments to the proper agencies.

2345 **Union Withholding and Benefits Payable**–Accumulated amounts withheld from employee's pay in accordance with a collective bargaining agreement. This account can also be used to accrue the employers' liability for union benefits such as pension and welfare, training, health insurance and other required benefits. To accrue benefits, credit this account and debit Account 4150 (Union benefits). Debit this account for payments to the Union or appropriate fund.

2350 **Sales and Use Tax Payable**–Credit amount of tax received from purchasers, and debit payments to the taxing authority. Note: Taxes paid on material used in construction are debited to Account 1430 (Direct construction cost) or Account 3830 (Building materials).

2360 **Real Estate Taxes Payable**–Credit the company's liability incurred to date, and debit payments to the taxing authority.

2370 **Income Taxes Payable**–Credit for accrual of the company's current liability for federal and state income and franchise taxes, and debit payments to the taxing authorities.

2390 **Accrued Interest Payable**–Credit interest accrued and payable, and debit payments.

2400 **Accrued Salaries and Wages Payable**–Control account for accrued salaries and wages. Credit accrued salaries and wages, and debit when payments are made.

2410 **Accrued Commissions Payable**–Commissions earned but not yet paid. Credit amount of commission due and debit payments.

2420 **Workers' Compensation Insurance Payable**–Amounts withheld from payment to subcontractors for workers' compensation insurance but not yet paid. This account can also be used to accrue the employers' liability for workers' compensation on their employees.

2425 **Other Accrued Expenses**–The liability for expenses that have been incurred but the invoices have not been received or the expense has not been paid, such as professional fees, bonuses, commissions, and vacations. Detailed accounts for detail accounts for other accrued expenses may be provided by using an additional subledger or a two-digit subclass to the main account number.

2430 **Deferred Income**–Advance payments made by tenants or other sources, for which income is not yet earned. Credit this account when an advance payment is received. Debit the account when the revenue is earned, and credit the appropriate income account.

2440 **Due to Affiliated Companies or Subsidiaries**–Amounts due to affiliated or subsidiary companies currently due.

2450 **Due to Officers, Stockholders, Owners**–Amounts due to officers, stockholders, owners, and partners currently due.

2480 **Billings in Excess of Costs**–This account is used mostly by remodelers, custom builders, and commercial builders to record charges that exceed their estimated costs (sometimes referred to as over billing) using the percentage of completion method of accounting.

2490 **Other Current Liabilities**– Miscellaneous current liabilities not otherwise classified

2500–2890 Long-Term Payable Liabilities

2510 **Long-Term Notes Payable**–Control account for notes on vehicles, equipment and other assets used in operations. Include current portion in Account 2240 (Current portion of long-term debt). Detailed accounts for long-term payable liabilities may be provided by using an additional subledger or a two-digit subclass to the main account number.

2530 **Mortgage Notes Payable**–Control account for mortgages on rental property and land, and buildings used in operations. Include current portion in Account 2240 (Current portion of long-term debt). Detailed accounts for mortgage notes payable may be provided by using an additional subledger or a two-digit subclass to the main account number.

2600 **Deferred Income Taxes Payable**–Income taxes due on deferred income.

2610 **Due to Affiliated Companies or Subsidiaries, Long-Term**–Amounts due to affiliated companies or subsidiaries that are to be carried for a long-term period.

2620 **Due to Officers, Stockholders, Owners, Long-Term, and partners**–Amounts due to company officers, stockholders, owners and partners to be carried for an long-term period of time.

2700 **Other Long-Term Liabilities**–Long-term liabilities not otherwise classified.

2900–2990 Owners' Equity

2900 **Common Stock**–Par value or stated value of stock outstanding.

2910 **Additional Paid in Capital**–Amounts received in excess of par or stated value of stock.

2920 **Retained Earnings**–Prior years' accumulation of profits.

2930 **Treasury Stock**–The corporation's own capital stock which has been issued and then reacquired by the corporation by either purchase or gift.

2940 **Unrealized Holding Loss**–Represents cumulative unrealized loss on investments or marketable securities.

Investments or marketable securities should be adjusted to their market values on an annual or periodic basis.

2950 **Partnership or Proprietorship Account**–Separate account for each partner, indicating accumulated equity to date. Detailed accounts for Partnership or Proprietorship Account may be provided by using an additional subledger or a two-digit subclass to the main account number.

2960 **Distributions, Dividends, and Draws**–Accumulated owners' withdrawals for period. Maintain a separate account for each owner. At the end of the fiscal year, the account should be closed and amounts transferred and debited to Account 2920 (Retained earnings) or 2950 (Partnership or proprietorship account) as applicable. Detailed accounts for Distributions, Dividends, and Draws may be provided by using an additional subledger or a two-digit subclass to the main account number.

3000–3990 Sales, Revenues, and Cost of Sales

3000–3490 Sales and Revenues

3000 **Sales, Land Held for Development**–Revenues earned from sales of raw land not yet subdivided and without improvements.

3050 **Sales, Developed Lots**–Revenues earned from sales of partially or fully developed lots.

3100 **Sales, Single-Family Speculative**–Revenues earned from sales of spec houses.

3110 **Sales, Single-Family Production**–Revenues earned from sales of production houses.

3120 **Sales, Single-Family Custom Designed**–Revenues earned from sales of custom houses.

3125 **Sales, Single-Family Custom, No Land**–Revenues earned from sales of houses built under contract on land owned by someone other than the builder.

3130 **Sales, Residential Remodeling**–Revenues earned from sales of residential remodeling work.

3133 **Sales, Commercial and Industrial Remodeling**–Revenues earned from sales of commercial and industrial remodeling work.

3135 **Sales, Insurance Restoration**–Revenues earned from sales of insurance restoration work.

3137 **Sales, Repairs**–Revenues earned from sales of repair work.

3140 **Sales, Multifamily**–Revenues earned from sales of multifamily units.

3150 **Sales, Commercial and Industrial**–Revenues earned from sales of new commercial and industrial construction.

3160 **Sales, Trade-Ins, and Repossessions**–Revenues earned from sales of houses originally received as partial payment on another sale or repossessed.

3190 **Sales, Other**–Revenues earned from sales of construction activities not otherwise classified.

3200 **Rental Property Income**–Revenues earned from rental of investment property and office space.

3210 **Common Area Reimbursements**–Revenues earned from tenant reimbursement of common area expenses. Common area expenses should be charged to the applicable account within the 7000 Series. Other reimbursements should be credited to Account 3220 (Other reimbursements).

3220 **Other Reimbursements**–Revenues earned from tenant reimbursement of expenses. Expenses incurred by the company should be charged to the applicable account within the 7000 Series.

3230 **Parking Fee Income**–Revenue earned from sales of the rental of company-owned parking facilities.

3240 **Amenities Facilities Income**–Revenue earned from rental and use charges for company-owned recreational facilities.

3360 **Construction Management Fee Income**–Revenues earned from construction management activities.

3379 **Design Fee Income**–Revenues earned from design activities.

3400 **Miscellaneous Income**–Revenues earned from sources not otherwise classified.

3410 **Interest Income**–Interest earned from certificates of deposits, savings accounts, and other sources.

3420 **Dividend Income**–Dividends earned from investments in stocks, bonds, and other sources

3450 **Earned Discounts**–Cash discounts earned from payment on account within the time established by the supplier or subcontractor.

3490 **Sales Concessions and Discounts**–This account records the difference between published sales price and the contract price. It is used to capture the impact of concessions on company margins. If this account is used, then the published price is placed in the appropriate sales account and concessions and discounts are debited here. This is a contra-account and thus a reduction to sales.

3500–3700 Cost of Sales

3500 **Cost of Sales, Land Held for Development**–Transfer from and credit Account 1320 (Land held for development) at the time of sale and debit Account 3500 (Cost of sales, land held for development).

3550 **Cost of Sales, Developed Lots**–Allocated amount to be written off on lots sold. Credit Account 1420 if the lot was developed prior to purchase or 1412 (Accumulated allocations, land and land development costs) if the company developed the lot, and debit Account 3550 (Cost of Sales, Developed Lots).

3600 **Cost of Sales, Single-Family Speculative**–Direct construction costs related to sales of homes recorded in account 3100 (Cost of Sales, single-family speculative). Transfer from and credit Account 1430 (Direct construction cost). Debit Account 3600.

3610 **Cost of Sales, Single-Family Production**–Direct construction costs of houses built under contract. Transfer from Account 1430 (Direct construction cost). Debit Account 3610 (Cost of sales, single-family production).

3620 **Cost of Sales, Single-Family Custom Designed**–Direct construction costs of custom houses. Transfer from Account 1430 (Direct construction cost) if applicable. Debit Account 3620 (Cost of sales, single-family custom designed).

3625 **Cost of Sales, Single-Family Custom, No Land**–Direct construction costs of custom homes built on land owned by someone other than the builder. Transfer from 1430 (Direct construction cost) if applicable. Debit Account 3625 (Cost of sales, single-family custom, no land).

3630 **Cost of Sales, Remodeling**–Direct construction costs of remodeling. Transfer from Account 1430 (Direct construction cost) if applicable. Debit Account 3630 (Cost of sales, remodeling). An alternative method is to use 3800 account series for directly posting remodeling costs to costs of sales.

3633 **Cost of Sales, Commercial and Industrial Remodeling**–Direct construction costs of commercial and industrial jobs. Transfer from Account 1430 (Direct construction cost) if applicable. Debit Account 3633 (Cost of sales, commercial and industrial remodeling).

3635 **Cost of Sales, Insurance Restoration**–Direct costs for insurance restoration work. Transfer from Account 1430 (Direct construction cost) if applicable. Debit Account 3635.

3637 **Cost of Sales, Repairs**–Direct costs for repairs. Transfer from Account 1430 (Direct construction cost) if applicable. Debit Account 3637 (Cost of sales, insurance restoration).

3640 **Cost of Sales, Multifamily**–Direct construction costs of multifamily units sold. Transfer from Account 1430 (Direct construction cost). Debit Account 3640 (Cost of sales, multifamily).

3650 **Cost of Sales, Commercial and Industrial**–Direct construction costs of commercial and industrial jobs. Transfer from Account 1430 (Direct construction cost) if applicable. Debit Account 3650 (Cost of sales, commercial and industrial).

3660 **Cost of Sales, Trade-Ins**–Trade-in allowance and refurbishing. Transfer from Account 1530 (Trade-ins and repossessions) at time of sale. Debit Account 3660 (Cost of sales, trade-ins).

3690 **Cost of Sales, Other**–Costs incurred to generate income from sources not otherwise classified.

3700 **Direct Construction Cost for Prior Periods**–Cost adjustments to cost of sales for charges or credits from prior periods closings. These adjustments are for changes in cost that have not been accounted for after closing of an individual unit.

3800–3899 Costs of Construction

The following accounts can be used by remodelers and builders for direct posting of construction costs to cost of sales instead of posting direct construction costs to account 1430 (Direct construction cost).

3810 **Direct Labor**–Include the gross wages paid to lead carpenters and crews engaged in the remodeling process.

3820 **Labor Burden**–Payroll taxes and workers compensation insurance as well as other items such as health insurance, life and disability insurance that relate to gross wages paid to the field crew. Also include vacation, holiday, sick and other paid days off for the field crew.

3830 **Building Material**–Cost of materials used on a remodeling project. Include all freight and taxes paid on the material in this account.

3840 **Subcontractors**–Cost of subcontractors used on a specific remodeling project.

3850 **Rental Equipment**–Cost of rental equipment used on a specific remodeling project.

3860 **Other Direct Costs**–Include costs of small tools consumed on a specific remodeling project, cost of permits and fees obtained for a particular project, and any other direct construction costs not otherwise classified.

3870 **Professional Design Fees**–Costs paid to architects, engineers, and interior designers, certified kitchen designers and bath designers for use on a specific remodeling job. Also include in-house design salaries, wages, and the related labor burden in this account if they are incurred on a specific remodeling job.

4000–4990 Indirect Construction Cost

The 4000 series of accounts is an alternative to Account 1440 (Indirect construction cost). The 4000 Series allows a detailed breakdown of accounts in the general ledger, while maintaining a four-digit numerical code. The indirect costs accumulated in these accounts must still be allocated to houses or specific jobs held in inventory in order to comply with GAAP and/or IRS regulations.

4000–4090 Salaries and Wages

Salaries and wages of personnel directly engaged in the construction process but not identified with a specific unit.

4010 **Superintendents**–Salaries of supervisory personnel for time spent in organizing, planning, or supervising production crews. This category does not include wages of personnel who work on specific jobs with their crews.

4020 **Laborers**–Wages paid to laborers on construction that cannot be charged to a specific job. Labor should be estimated, budgeted, and charged to a specific job if possible.

4030 **Project and Production Managers**–Salaries paid to supervisors of superintendents.

4040 **Architects, Drafters, Estimators, and Purchasers**–Salaries and wages of persons who perform these duties for construction jobs. If area is department to itself, each person's job may be broken down into a separate account.

4050 **Warranty and Customer Service Managers**–Salaries of employees responsible for the warranty and service function.

4060 **Warranty and Customer Service Wages**–Labor incurred to repair, replace, or service any item after possession by owner on a particular unit.

4070 **Other Indirect Construction Wages**–Salaries and wages of personnel, such as timekeepers, security guards, and/or quality control inspectors, involved in the construction process but not identified with specific units.

4110–4190 Payroll Taxes and Benefits

4110 **Payroll Taxes**–Accumulated share of FICA, unemployment, Medicare, social security, and other company paid taxes relating to salaries and wages charged as indirect cost.

4120 **Workers' Compensation Insurance**–Insurance premiums for individual construction workers.

4130 **Health and Accident Insurance**–Premiums for health and accident insurance for indirect construction workers.

4140 **Retirement, Pension, and Profit Sharing**–Employer contributions to retirement, pension, and profit-sharing plans for indirect construction workers.

4150 **Union Benefits**–Benefits related to indirect construction workers in accordance with a collective bargaining agreement.

4190 **Other Benefits**–Benefits relating to salaries and wages charged as indirect costs not otherwise classified.

4200–4290 Field Office Expenses

Maintenance and repairs, utilities, telephone, and other expenses incidental to a field office, including erection and moving. The field office is often a trailer. If the office is in model, include these expenses in 6600 accounts (Model Home Expenses).

4210 **Rent, Field Office**–Rent of field office.

4230 **Repairs and Maintenance, Field Office**–Repairs and maintenance, including service contracts, of field office.

4250 **Utilities, Field Office**–Heat, electricity, and other utilities for field office.

4260 **Telephone, Field Office**–Installation and monthly charges for field office telephone and related communications equipment.

4265 **Mobile Phones, Pagers, and Radios**–Purchase and monthly charges for cellular phones, pagers, and field radios for construction personnel.

4290 **Other Field Office Expenses**–Other expenses for field office not included in other categories.

4300–4390 Warehouse and Storage Expense

Costs incurred in material handling and storage if materials are not delivered to the job site by supplier.

4310 **Rent, Warehouse and Storage**–Rent on warehouse and storage facilities.

4330 **Repairs and Maintenance, Warehouse and Storage**–Repairs and maintenance, including service contracts, of warehouse and storage facilities.

4350 **Utilities, Warehouse and Storage**–Heat, electricity and other utilities for warehouse and storage facilities.

4360 **Telephone, Warehouse and Storage**–Installation and monthly charges of telephone in warehouse and storage.

4400–4490 Construction Vehicles, Travel, and Entertainment

4410 **Lease Payments, Construction Vehicles**–Payments on leased or rented vehicles used by construction personnel.

4420 **Mileage Reimbursement**–Payment to field personnel for use of their private vehicles.

4430 **Repairs and Maintenance, Construction Vehicles**–Repair and maintenance costs for automobiles and trucks used by construction personnel including minor repairs and major overhauls.

4440 **Operating Expenses, Construction Vehicles**–Fuel, oil, and lubrication expenses for automobiles and trucks used by construction personnel.

4450 **Taxes, Licenses, Insurance, Construction Vehicles**–Property damage and liability insurance, licenses, fees, and taxes on vehicles used by construction personnel.

4460 **Travel, Construction Department**–Travel expense incurred by construction personnel.

4470 **Customer Business Entertainment, Construction**–Business related entertainment expenses incurred by construction personnel.

4480 **Training and Education, Construction**–Training and education expenses incurred by construction personnel.

4490 **Recruiting Fees and Expenses, Construction Personnel**–Expenses associated with the hiring of construction personnel.

4500–4590 Construction Equipment

Costs of maintaining and operating construction equipment.

4510 **Rent, Construction Equipment**–Payments on leased or rented equipment.

4530 **Repairs and Maintenance, Construction Equipment**–Repair and maintenance costs on equipment.

4540 **Operating Expenses, Construction Equipment**–Fuel, oil, and lubrication expenses on equipment.

4550 **Taxes and Insurance, Construction Equipment**–Taxes and insurance required on equipment.

4560 **Small Tools and Supplies**–Cost of items such as hand tools, shovels, skill saws, small power tools, and extension cords used in construction.

4600–4690 Expenses for Maintaining Unsold Units and Units under Construction

Costs applicable to units under construction until delivered to customer.

4610 **Temporary Utilities**–Utility hook-up costs and utility bills related to units under construction. Custom and small-volume builders may consider classifying these costs as part of direct construction costs.

4620 **Trash Maintenance**–Cost of trash hauling, dumpsters, and other equipment to maintain construction site.

4640 **Lawn Care**–Costs required to maintain the lawn prior to transfer to customer.

4650 **Utilities, Completed Units**–Utility cost and hookups for finished units held in inventory and awaiting sale.

4660 **Repairs and Maintenance, Completed Units**–Cost of repair and maintenance to any unit held in inventory for sale.

4700–4790 Warranty and Customer Service

4710 **Salaries and Wages, Warranty**–Labor incurred to repair, replace, or service any item after possession by owner on a particular unit.

4720 **Materials, Warranty**–Price of materials to repair, replace, or service any item after possession by owner on a particular unit.

4730 **Subcontractor, Warranty**–Cost of subcontractor incurred to repair, replace, or service any item after possession by owner on a particular unit.

4790 **Other Warranty Expenses**–Costs other than labor, materials, or subcontractors incurred to repair, replace, or service any item after possession by owner on a particular unit.

4800–4890 Depreciation Expenses

4820 **Depreciation, Construction Office**–Depreciation on construction office equipment.

4830 **Depreciation, Warehouse**–Depreciation of warehouse.

4840 **Depreciation, Construction Vehicle**–Depreciation expenses of construction vehicles.

4850 **Depreciation, Construction Equipment**–Depreciation expenses of construction equipment.

4900–4990 Other

4910 **Insurance and Bonding Expenses**–Cost of obtaining insurance or bonding for construction projects and properties.

4920 **Builders Risk Insurance**–Cost of obtaining builders risk insurance. Custom and small volume builders may be more inclined to treat this as a direct cost.

4990 **Absorbed Indirect Costs**–In order to comply with IRS and GAAP requirements this is a contra account used to allocate the proportional share of indirect construction costs to work in process inventories. This contra account requires a year-end closing adjustment, which is usually handled by an accountant.

5000–5990 Financing Expenses

5000–5090 Interest

5010 **Interest on Line of Credit**–Interest expense on loans held by banks and other lenders for operating capital.

5020 **Interest on Notes Payable**–Interest expense on notes payable for fixed assets such as office buildings and vehicles.

5030 **Interest Expense on Developed Lots**–Interest expense on developed lots not currently under construction.

5040 **Interest Incurred on Construction Loans**–Interest expense paid during the building of a house. In order to comply with IRS and GAAP requirements, interest on construction loans must be capitalized during the period of construction. If interest is posted to this account, to comply with IRS and GAAP requirements, allocate the proportionate share of interest to work in process inventories.

5050 **Interest on Completed Inventory**–Interest expense paid after completion of construction and before closing of the unit.

5090 **Interest Expense, Other**–Other interest paid or accrued.

5100–5190 Construction Loan Points and Fees

5120 **Points and Fees**–Expenses paid on points and fees for construction loans.

5130 **Appraisal and Related Fees**–Service charges paid for appraisal of property relating to construction loans.

5140 **Inspection Fees**–Fees for inspection by lenders.

5200–5290 Closing Costs

Closing costs related to the sale of finished houses.

5210 **Closing Costs**–Closing costs related to the sale of finished houses, usually paid by the seller. Custom and small-volume builders may charge this as a direct expense. If paid on buyer's behalf as concession, include in account 6930 (Sales concessions).

5220 **Title and Recording**–Fees charged for searching and recording, and for title insurance.

5230 **Loan Fees**–Origination or standby fees on permanent financing commitments.

6000–6990 Sales and Marketing Expenses

This section of the operating expense chart of accounts is reserved for sales and marketing expenses that may be written off as period expenses.

6000–6090 Sales Salaries and Commissions

6010 **Sales Manager's Compensation**–Compensation, including bonuses or incentives, for sales managers.

6030 **Salaries, Sales Personnel**–Salaries for non-commission activities, excluding draws against present or future commissions.

6040 **Sales Commissions, In-house**–Commissions paid to employees. Remodelers sometimes charge this as a direct cost.

6050 **Sales Commissions, Outside**–Commissions paid to sales agents and others not employed by the company.

6090 **Other Sales Office Salaries**–Salaries and Wages for clerical and other personnel who work directly for the sales department or sales office.

6100–6190 Payroll Taxes and Benefits, Sales and Marketing

Payroll taxes and benefits associated with Salaries and Wages of the sales and marketing department or sales office employees.

6110 **Payroll Taxes, Sales and Marketing**–Accumulated share of FICA, unemployment, and other taxes relating to salaries and wages of sales and marketing personnel.

6120 **Workers' Compensation Insurance, Sales and Marketing**–Insurance premiums on salaries and wages of sales and marketing personnel.

6130 **Health and Accident Insurance, Sales and Marketing**–Premiums for health and accident insurance for sales and marketing personnel.

6140 **Retirement, Pension, and Profit-Sharing Plans, Sales and Marketing**–Employer contributions paid to retirement, pension, and profit-sharing plans for sales and marketing personnel.

6190 **Other Benefits**–Benefits relating to salaries and wages of sales and marketing personnel.

6200–6290 Sales Office Expenses

Operating costs relating to a separate sales office or design center. If sales office is in a model, include expenses in the 6660–6690 account series (Model Home Maintenance).

6210 **Rent, Sales Office**–Rental of sales office.

6230 **Repairs and Maintenance, Sales Office**–Cost of all interior and exterior sales office building repairs and maintenance, including interior remodeling not capitalized, janitorial service, landscaping, and window washing.

6250 **Utilities, Sales Office**–Heat and other utilities for sales office.

6260 **Telephone, Sales Office**–Installation and monthly charges for sales office. Both land-line and cell phones.

6270 **Supplies, Sales Office**–Office supplies used by sales office staff.

6300–6390 Advertising and Sales Promotion

6310 **Print Advertising**–Classified and display advertising expenses.

6320 **Radio Advertising**–Expenses for radio time and related services.

6325 **Television Advertising**–Expenses for television time and related services.

6330 **Internet Fees, Web Page Design and Maintenance Costs**–Expenses for Internet fees, design of World Wide Web pages and related maintenance fees.

6340 **Brochures and Catalogues**–Cost of designing and printing brochures and catalogues.

6350 **Signs**–Photography, typography, printing, artwork, copy writing, materials, and supply expenses required to make signs.

6355 **Billboards**–Fees paid for art and advertising on billboards.

6365 **Promotions**–Fees paid for special programs, e.g., move-in gifts.

6370 **Agency Commissions**–Fees paid to agencies that assist in setting up advertising programs.

6380 **Multiple Listing Fees**–Payments to a centralized brokerage service.

6390 **Public Relations**–Fees paid to public relations firms for press releases and other publicity.

6395 **Referral Fees**–Payments for referrals.

6400–6490 Sales Vehicles, Travel, and Entertainment

6410 **Lease Payment, Sales Vehicles**–Payments on leased or rented vehicles used for sales and marketing personnel.

6420 **Mileage Reimbursement, Sales and Marketing**–Payment to sales and marketing personnel for use of their private vehicles.

6430 **Repairs and Maintenance, Sales Vehicles**–Repair and maintenance costs of the company's automobiles used by sales and marketing personnel, including minor repairs and major overhauls.

6440 **Operating Expense, Sales and Marketing Vehicles**–Fuel, oil, and lubrication costs.

6450 **Taxes, Licenses, Insurance, Sales and Marketing Vehicles**–Property damage and liability insurance, licenses, fees, and taxes on the company's vehicles used by sales and marketing personnel.

6460 **Travel, Sales and Marketing**–Travel expenses incurred by sales and marketing personnel.

6470 **Customer Business Entertainment, Sales and Marketing**–Entertainment expenses incurred by sales and marketing personnel.

6600–6690 Model Home Maintenance

6610 **Rent or Lease Payments, Model Home Furnishings**–Costs of renting or leasing model home furnishings.

6620 **Rent or Lease Payments, Model Home**–Costs of renting or leasing the model home.

6625 **Decorating Fees, Model Home**–Fee for decorating services.

6630 **Repairs and Maintenance, Model Homes**–Repairs maintenance and decoration expenses resulting from use, damage, or minor changes to the model or its furnishings.

6650 **Utilities, Model Homes**–Heat, electricity, water, and sewer expenses.

6670 **Lawn and Landscaping Care, Model Homes**–Labor and material costs for lawn cutting and for watering, seeding, fertilizing, and pruning lawn and other plantings.

6680 **Cleanup, Model Homes**–Costs relating to window washing and daily cleanup.

6690 **Interest on Model Homes**–Interest paid after completion of the model home(s).

6700–6790 Sales and Marketing Fees

6710 **Market Research and Consultation**–Fees for market research and consultation.

6720 **Interior Design Fee**–Fees paid for outside designer to assist buyers with their selections.

6770 **Recruiting Fees and Expenses, Sales and Marketing Personnel**–Expenses associated with the hiring of sales and marketing personnel.

6780 **Training and Education Expenses**–Cost of travel, registration fees for seminars and conventions, hotel and lodging expenses, in-house programs, literature, and materials. Also include expenses incurred for conventions and trade shows as well as national, state, and local association meetings.

6800–6890 Depreciation

6810 **Depreciation, Sales Office**–Depreciation on sales office.

6830 **Depreciation, Sales Vehicles**–Depreciation on sales and marketing vehicles.

6870 **Depreciation, Model Home Furnishings and Decorations**–Depreciation on model home furnishings and decorations.

6900–6990 Other Marketing Expense

6930 **Sales Concessions**–Announced discounts, rebates, and other incentives (such as gifts and travel incentives) provided to customers as part of marketing and sales strategy.

6940 **Buydowns**–Refunds of interest and points issued to customers in the sales process.

6999 **Other Sales and Marketing Expenses**–Sales and Marketing expenses not otherwise classified.

7000–7990 Operating and Management Expense, Rental Operations

7000–7090 Property Management Salaries and Wages

7010 **Property Manager's Compensation**–Compensation, including bonuses or incentives, for managers of property management personnel.

7030 **Salaries and Wages, Property Management Personnel**–Direct Salaries and Wages for non-commission activities, excluding draws against present and future commissions, which should be debited to Account 7040 (Commissions, in-house) or Account 7050 (Commissions, outside).

7040 **Commissions, In-House**–Commissions paid to property management personnel employed by the company for leasing of rental property.

7050 **Commissions, Outside**–Commissions paid to sales agents and others not employed by the company for leasing of rental property.

7060 **Salaries and Wages to Maintenance Personnel**–Wages and salaries of company personnel assigned to maintenance and repair of rental property. In order to track different type of work performed by maintenance personnel (i.e. janitorial service, landscaping, repair) you may want to add a 1 or 2 digit prefix for each type of work performed.

7070 **Payroll Taxes and Benefits, Rental Operations**–Cost of the company's FICA, Medicare, and federal and state unemployment insurance for rental personnel.

7072 **Workers' Compensation Insurance, Rental**–Insurance premiums on salaries and wages of rental personnel.

7073 **Health and Accident Insurance, Rental**–Premiums for health and accident insurance for rental personnel.

7074 **Retirement, Pension, and Profit-Sharing Plans, Rental**–Employer contributions to retirement, pension, and profit-sharing plans for rental personnel.

7079 **Other Benefits Rental**–Salaries and Wages for in-house clerical and other personnel involved in property management activities, not otherwise classified.

7100–7190 Rental Expenses

7110 **Advertising**–Costs for advertising directly related to renting individual rental units.

7130 **Credit Reports**–Charges from credit bureaus for reports on prospective tenants.

7190 **Other Rental Expenses**–Rental expenses not otherwise classified, such as concessions to tenants.

7200–7290 Administrative Expense, Rental Operations

7220 **Management and Service Fees**–Fees paid to outside firms for the management and operation of a company-owned property management activity.

7230 **Office Expenses**–Costs for maintaining an office for a property management activity, including rent, supplies, and postage.

7240 **Telephone**–Costs of the standard monthly charges and long distance calls directly related to a property management activity.

7250 **Tenant Bad Debts**–Write-off of past-due rents receivable from tenants.

7260 **Collection Costs**–Costs incurred in pursuing collection of past-due rents receivable, including collection agency fees.

7290 **Other Administrative Expenses**–Administrative expenses of a property management activity not otherwise classified.

7300–7390 Professional Services, Rental Operations

7310 **Legal Services**–Charges for legal counsel for all services relating to a property management activity.

7320 **Accounting Services**–Charges for preparation of financial statements, tax advice, and other services rendered by an outside accounting firm relating to a property management activity.

7330 **Market Research**–Charges from consulting firms or individuals for market research relating to a property management activity.

7390 **Other Professional Services, Rental Operations**–Professional service costs for a property management activity not otherwise classified.

7400–7490 Operating Expense, Rental Operations

7410 **Utilities**–Gas, electricity, water and sewer service, and other utilities for rental buildings.

7420 **Engineering**–Payroll and other costs associated with engineering activity related to property management.

7430 **Janitorial**–Costs for janitorial services for property management activity.

7440 **Trash Removal Service**–Costs of contracted services for the removal of trash and other waste from related buildings.

7450 **Exterminating**–Supplies and other costs associated with exterminating services supplied by the company's personnel or an independent contractor.

7460 **Snow Removal**–Supplies and other costs associated with snow removal services supplied by the company's personnel or an independent contractor.

7470 **Other Contractual Services**–Costs of services such as sign painting and design provided under contract for a property management activity and not otherwise classified.

7480 **Motor Vehicles and Equipment, Rental Operations**–Cost of leasing and operating equipment for use at the rental property.

7490 **Other Rental Operations Expenses**–Operating costs of a rental property not otherwise classified.

7500–7590 Taxes and Insurance, Rental Operations

7510 **Real Estate Property Taxes**–Local taxes on rental property land, improvements, and buildings.

7520 **Personal Property Taxes**–Local taxes assessed on business-owned personal property at a rental property.

7530 **Franchise Taxes**–State tax on rental property for privilege of doing business.

7540 **License Fees**–Local fees for licenses, registrations, and permits.

7570 **Insurance, Rental Operations**–Costs for general liability, property damage, and extended fire insurance.

7590 **Other Taxes and Insurance, Rental Operations**–Tax and insurance costs not otherwise classified.

7600–7690 Maintenance and Repair Expense, Rental Operations

7610 **Tenant Redecorating**–Payroll, supplies, and all other costs associated with redecorating rental units, including services supplied by the company's personnel or independent contractors.

7630 **Maintenance Contracts and Services**–Charges from independent contractors for maintenance and repair services.

7640 **Ground Maintenance and Repairs**–Costs of maintaining rental property grounds, including landscaping provided by the company's personnel or an independent contractor.

7650 **Vehicle Maintenance and Repairs, Rental Operations**–Labor and material costs associated with the general maintenance and repair of the company's motor vehicles used at a rental property.

7660 **Equipment Maintenance and Repairs, Rental Operations**–Labor and materials costs incurred by the company's personnel or an outside contractor for the maintenance and repair of equipment used at a rental property.

7670 **Recreational Facilities Maintenance and Repairs**–Labor and materials costs incurred by the company's personnel or an outside contractor for the maintenance and repair of recreational facilities at a rental property.

7700–7790 Financing Expenses, Rental Operations

7710 **Interest on Mortgage Payable**–Interest charges associated with the permanent mortgage loan on rental buildings.

7720 **Interest on Notes Payable**–Interest charges associated with notes payable associated with rental operations.

7800–7890 Depreciation Expense, Rental Operations

7810 **Depreciation, Building**–Depreciation for buildings such as rental properties.

7820 **Depreciation, Maintenance Equipment**–Depreciation for company-owned equipment used for maintaining rental premises.

7830 **Depreciation, Vehicles**–Depreciation for company-owned vehicles and maintenance equipment used at rental properties.

7840 **Depreciation, Furniture and Fixtures**–Depreciation for company-owned furniture, fixtures, office machines, and office equipment used at for rental operations.

7850 **Depreciation, Amenities**–Depreciation for rental property recreational facilities.

7890 **Other Depreciation**–Depreciation for assets not otherwise classified used in rental operations.

7900–7990 Other Management and Operating Expenses

Management and operating expenses not otherwise classified.

8000–8990 General and Administrative Expenses

8000–8090 **Salaries, Wages, and Bonuses**

8010 **Salaries, Owners**–Total compensation paid to owners including salaries, and bonuses.

8020 **Salaries, Officers**–Total compensation paid to company officers who are not company owners including salaries, and bonuses.

8030 **Salaries, Management**–Total compensation paid to upper- and middle-management personnel other than owners or officers including salaries, and bonuses.

8050 **Salaries and Wages, Office and Clerical**–Total compensation paid to clerical and other personnel below the managerial level including salaries, wages, and bonuses.

8090 **Other General and Administrative Salaries and Wages**–Total compensation paid to general and administrative personnel and those not otherwise classified including salaries, wages, and bonuses.

8100–8190 Payroll Taxes and Benefits

8110 **Payroll Taxes–**Cost of the company's FICA, Medicare, federal and state unemployment insurance, and other local taxes that relate to administrative salaries and wages.

8120 **Workers' Compensation Insurance**–Insurance premiums for workers' compensation paid by the employer for administrative and hourly employees.

8130 **Health and Accident Insurance**–Health and accident insurance premiums paid by the employer for administrative personnel.

8140 **Retirement, Pension, and Profit-Sharing Plans**–Employee contributions to retirement, pension, and profit-sharing plans for administrative personnel.

8190 **Other Employee Benefits**–Benefits relating to salaries and wages of administrative personnel.

8200–8290 Office Expense

8210 **Rent**–Rental payments for administrative office space.

8220 **Office Equipment Rental**–Rental payments on office equipment, cellular phones, and pagers for office personnel.

8230 **Repairs and Maintenance, Administrative Office Space**–Cost of all interior and exterior administrative office building repairs and maintenance, including interior remodeling not capitalized, janitorial service, landscaping, and window washing.

8240 **Repairs and Maintenance, Administrative Office Equipment**– All contracts and other charges for maintenance of office equipment.

8250 **Utilities, Administrative Office**–Cost of utilities that serve the administrative offices.

8260 **Telephone, Administrative Office**–Standard monthly fees and long distance charges, including cell phones, not applied to other functions or departments.

8270 **Office Supplies, Administrative Office**–Printing, stationery, and other office supplies.

8280 **Postage and Deliveries–**Stamps, express mail, couriers, FedEx, UPS, and other delivery services.

8290 **Miscellaneous Expenses, Administrative Office**–Office expenses not otherwise classified, including answering service monthly fees, paging services.

8300–8390 Computer Expenses

8310 **Computer Supplies**–Paper, ribbons, and miscellaneous supplies necessary to the operation of the computer system.

8320 **Leases, Computer Hardware**–Lease payments on leased hardware.

8330 **Leases, Computer Software**–Lease payments on leased software.

8350 **Repairs and Maintenance, Computer Equipment**–Service contract or other payments for the maintenance of computer hardware.

8360 **Maintenance, Computer Software**–Contract or other payments for the maintenance agreement of the systems software.

8400–8490 Vehicle, Travel, and Entertainment

8410 **Lease, Administrative Vehicles**–Payments on leased or rental vehicles used by administrative personnel.

8420 **Mileage Reimbursement**–Payments to administrative personnel for use of their private vehicles.

8430 **Repairs and Maintenance, Administrative Vehicles**–Repair and maintenance costs of automobiles used by administrative personnel, including minor repairs and major overhauls.

8440 **Operating Expense, Administrative Vehicles**–Vehicle fuel, oil, and lubrication costs.

8450 **Taxes, Licenses, and Insurance, Administrative Vehicles**–Taxes, licenses, fees, and property damage and liability insurance on vehicles used by administrative personnel.

8460 **Travel**–Travel expenses incurred by administrative personnel.

8470 **Customer Business Expense**–Entertainment expenses incurred by administrative personnel.

8480 **Meeting Expenses**–Expenses incurred by officers and employees representing the company before groups, industry meetings, or other outside events.

8490 **In-House Meeting Expenses**–Expenses incurred in providing in-house meetings.

8500–8590 Taxes

8510 **Sales-and-Use Taxes**–Taxes imposed by states, counties, and cities on non direct construction cost materials used within the city limits but purchased outside those boundaries.

8520 **Real Estate Taxes**–Tax on property used for the company's offices, and realty taxes not charged elsewhere.

8530 **Personal Property Taxes**–Assessment of personal property owned by the company.

8540 **License Fees**–License, registration, municipal fees, and operating permits.

8590 **Other Taxes**–Taxes not otherwise classified, such as state tax on capitalization and franchise tax.

8600–8690 Insurance

8610 **Hazard Insurance/Property Insurance**–Fire and extended coverage on buildings and contents.

8630 **General Liability Insurance**–Costs of liability insurance other than vehicles, including general and product liability insurance.

8690 **Other Insurance**–Insurance premiums not otherwise classified.

8700–8790 Professional Services

8710 **Accounting Services**–Audit charges and charges for assistance in the preparation of financial statements, tax advice, and other services rendered by an outside accounting firm.

8720 **Legal Services**–Charges submitted by legal counsel for services rendered.

8730 **Consulting Services**–Service bureau, timesharing, or professional fees for services rendered.

8770 **Recruiting and Hiring**–Expenses associated with hiring administrative personnel.

8790 **Other Professional Expenses**–Professional fees not otherwise classified.

8800–8890 Depreciation Expenses

8810 **Depreciation, Buildings**–Depreciation on company buildings such as administrative offices.

8830 **Depreciation, Vehicles**–Depreciation on company-owned vehicles used by administrative personnel.

8840 **Depreciation, Furniture, and Equipment**–Depreciation on furniture, fixtures, office machines, and other equipment.

8860 **Amortization of Leasehold Improvement**–Amortization of improvements to office buildings leased from another entity.

8870 **Depreciation, Computer Equipment and Software**–Deprecation for computer hardware and software programs. These may be segregated for easier tracking and control.

8880 **Amortization of Organization Cost**–Write-off of organization cost, including legal fees and corporate charter fees.

8890 **Depreciation, Other**–Depreciation and amortization charges not otherwise classified.

8900–8990 General and Administrative Expense, Other

8900 **Bad Debts**–Charge for uncollectible amounts on receivables. Credit goes to Account 1290, Allowance for Doubtful Accounts.

8910 **Contributions**–All charitable donations.

8911 **Contributions, Political**–All contributions made to political organizations and candidates. These contributions are generally not deductible.

8920 **Dues and Subscriptions**–Trade association dues and subscriptions for magazines, newspapers, trade journals, business publications, reports, and manuals.

8950 **Bank Charges**–Bank fees for miscellaneous charges. Check printing should be charged to Account 8270, Office Supplies.

8960 **Penalties and Other Nondeductible Expenses**–Tax penalties, fines, parking tickets.

8990 **Training and Education Expenses**–Cost of travel, registration fees for seminars and conventions, hotel and lodging expenses, in-house programs, literature, and materials. Also include expenses incurred for conventions and trade shows as well as national, state, and local association meetings.

9000–9990 Other Income and Expenses

9100–9190 Other Income

Income derived from sources other than the main activity of the business.

9100 **Income from Partnerships, Joint Ventures, S-Corps, and LLCs**–Income (loss) from participation in partnerships, joint ventures, S-Corps and LLCs.

9150 **Gain or Loss on Sale of Assets**–Gain or loss (debit) on the sale of assets that had been used in the operation of the business such as motor vehicles, computers, and office equipment.

9190 **Other**–Income derived from sources other than the main activity of the business, including speaking and consulting fees, expert witness fees, home inspections, real estate, budgeting fees.

9200–9290 Other Expenses

Extraordinary expenses or expenses attributable to activities not relating to the main activity of the business.

9200 **Extraordinary Expenses**–Expenses attributable to activities not relating to the main activity of the business. Separate account numbers within this series can be set up to track different categories of other expenses.

9300–9390 Provision for Income Taxes

Provision for federal and state taxes on current income.

9300 **Provision for Federal Income Taxes.**

9320 **Provision for State Income Taxes.**

9330 **Provision for Local Income Taxes.**

Part C. Basic Accounts for Small-Volume Builders

The following abbreviated list of accounts provides an example of the accounts typically used by small-volume builders, who build less than 25 units per year. The complete NAHB Chart of Accounts shown in Appendixes A and B contains more accounts than are normally required to perform the accounting function of the small construction firm. The listing below is a guide that small-volume builders may use to establish their own chart of accounts. The numerical codes and accounting categories listed below are compatible with those used in the complete NAHB Chart of Accounts.

1000–1990 Assets

1010 Petty cash
1020 Cash on deposit
1210 Accounts receivable, trade
1230 Notes receivable, trade
1260 Due on construction and development loans
1320 Land held for development
1410 Land and land development cost
1420 Developed lots

1430	Direct construction cost
1440	Indirect construction cost
1450	Direct construction cost–remodeling
1460	Accumulated allocation land and land development costs
1510	Finished units
1520	Trade-ins
1610	Refundable deposits
1620	Prepaid expenses
1630	Employee Advances
1650	Due from affiliated companies or subsidiaries, long-term
1690	Other current assets
1710	Investments, long-term
1810	Land
1820	Buildings
1830	Office furniture and equipment
1840	Vehicles
1850	Construction equipment
1920	Accumulated depreciation, buildings
1930	Accumulated depreciation, furniture and equipment
1940	Accumulated depreciation, vehicles
1950	Accumulated depreciation, construction equipment

2000–2990	**Liabilities and Owners' Equity**
2010	Contract deposits
2110	Accounts payable, trade
2210	Notes payable, trade
2310	Social Security (FICA-Medicare) tax payable
2320	Federal withholdings
2330	State withholdings
2340	Other payroll withholdings
2370	Income taxes payable
2450	Due to officers, stockholders, owners
2510	Long-term notes payable
2520	Development and construction loans payable
2900	Common stock
2910	Additional paid in capital
2920	Retained earnings
2950	Partnership and proprietorship

2960 Drawings

3000–3990 Sales, Revenues, and Cost of Sales

3050 Sales, developed lots
3100 Sales, single-family speculative
3110 Sales, single-family production
3120 Sales, single-family custom-designed
3130 Sales, remodeling
3140 Sales, multifamily
3160 Sales, trade-ins
3190 Sales, other
3550 Cost of sales, developed lots
3600 Cost of sales, single-family speculative
3610 Cost of sales, single-family production
3620 Cost of sales, single-family custom-designed
3630 Cost of sales, remodeling
3640 Cost of sales, multifamily
3660 Cost of sales, trade-ins
3690 Cost of sales, other

4000–4990 Indirect Construction Cost, Construction Overhead

5000–5990 Financing Expenses

6000–6990 Marketing Expenses

8000–8990 General and Administrative Expenses

8010 Salaries, owners
8020 Salaries, officers
8050 Salaries, office and clerical
8100 Payroll taxes and benefits
8200 Office expense
8300 Computer expenses
8400 Vehicle and travel
8470 Customer business entertainment
8500 Taxes
8600 Insurance

8700 Professional fees
8800 Depreciation expense
8900 Other general and administrative expenses

9000–9990 Other
9100 Other income
9200 Other expenses
9300 Provision for income taxes

Part D. Direct Construction Costs Subsidiary Ledger

General Ledger Account 143

1000–1999 Preparation Preliminaries
1000 Permits and Fees
1100 Architectural and Engineering
1200 Site Work
1300 Demolition
1400 Utility Connections
1500 Construction Period Financing Costs

2000–2999 Excavation and Foundation
2000 Excavation and backfill

3000–3999 Rough Structure
3000 Structural Steel
3100 Framing
3105 Framing Material
3110 Materials, Floor Framing
3120 Materials, Partition and Wall Framing
3130 Materials, Roof Framing
3140 Materials, Basement Framing
3150 Framing Labor
3400 Concrete
3500 Rough Sheet Metal
3600 Plumbing Total Contract (if used you will not need 5600 series)
3700 Electrical Total Contract (if used you will not need 5700 series)
3800 HVAC Total Contract (if used you will not need 5800 series)

4000–4999	**Full Enclosures**
4000	Roofing
4100	Masonry
4105	Masonry Materials
4110	Chimney
4120	Fireplace
4130	Brick veneer
4140	Brick or Stone Wall
4150	Masonry flooring
4500	Windows and Doors
4700	Insulation
4800	Exterior Trim
4900	Exterior painting

5000–5999	**Finishing Trades**
5000	Drywall
5100	Flooring
5200	Trim Carpentry
5300	Ceramic Tile
5400	Cabinets and Vanities
5600	Finish Plumbing
5700	Finish Electrical
5800	Finish HVAC
5900	Interior Decoration

6000–6999	**Completion and Inspection**
6000	Building Clean-Up
6100	Landscaping
6200	Driveway Contract Total
6300	Exterior Structures
6400	Walk-Through Inspection Checklist Costs

Part E. Indirect Construction Costs Subsidiary Ledger

General Ledger Account 1440

4000–4990	**Indirect Construction Cost**
4000–4090	**Salaries and Wages**
4010	Superintendents

4020	Laborers
4030	Production manager
4040	Architects, drafters, estimators, and purchasers
4050	Other indirect construction wages

4100–4190	**Payroll Taxes and Benefits**
4110	Payroll taxes
4120	Workers' compensation insurance
4130	Health and accident insurance
4140	Retirement, pension, and profit sharing
4150	Union benefits
4190	Other benefits

4200–4290	**Field Office Expenses**
4210	Rent, field office
4230	Repairs and maintenance, field office
4250	Utilities, field office
4260	Telephone, field office
4265	Mobile phones, pagers, and radios
4290	Other field office expenses

4300–4390	**Field Warehouse and Storage Expenses**
4310	Rent, field warehouse and storage
4330	Repairs and maintenance, field warehouse and storage
4350	Utilities, field warehouse and storage
4360	Telephone, field warehouse and storage

4400–4490	**Construction Vehicles, Travel, and Entertainment**
4410	Lease payments, construction vehicles
4420	Mileage reimbursement
4430	Repairs and maintenance, construction vehicles
4440	Operating expenses, construction vehicles
4450	Taxes, licenses, and insurance, construction vehicles
4460	Travel, construction department
4470	Customer business entertainment, construction
4480	Training and education, construction
4490	Recruiting fees and expenses, construction

4500–4590	**Construction Equipment**
4510	Rent, construction equipment
4530	Repairs and maintenance, construction equipment
4540	Operating expenses, construction equipment
4550	Taxes and insurance, construction equipment
4560	Small tools and supplies
4600–4690	**Expenses for Maintaining Unsold Units and Units Under Construction**
4610	Temporary utilities
4620	Trash maintenance
4640	Lawn care
4650	Utilities, completed units
4660	Repairs and maintenance, completed units
4700–4790	**Warranty and Customer Service**
4710	Salaries and wages, warranty
4720	Material, warranty
4730	Subcontractor, warranty
4790	Other, warranty expenses
4800–4890	**Depreciation Expenses**
4820	Depreciation, construction office
4830	Depreciation, warehouse
4840	Depreciation, construction vehicles
4850	Depreciation, construction equipment
4900–4990	**Other**
4910	Insurance and bonding expenses
4920	Builders risk insurance
4990	Absorbed indirect costs

Part F. Land Development Costs Subsidiary Ledger

General Ledger Account 141

0100	**Preacquisition costs**
0101	Options

0102	Fees
0103	Professional services
0110	**Acquisition costs**
0111	Purchase price undeveloped land
0112	Sales commissions
0113	Legal fees
0114	Appraisals
0115	Closing costs
0116	Interest and financing fees
0120	**Land Planning and Design**
0121	Bonds
0122	Fees
0123	Permits
0130	Engineering
0131	Civil engineering
0132	Soil testing
0133	Traffic engineering
0140	**Earthwork**
0141	Fill dirt
0142	Clearing lot
0143	Rock removal
0144	Erosion control
0145	Dust control
0150	**Utilities**
0151	Sewer lines
0152	Storm sewer
0153	Water lines
0154	Gas lines
0155	Electric lines
0156	Telephone lines
0157	Cable television lines
0160	**Streets and Walks**
0161	Curbs and gutters
0162	Walkways

0163	Paving
0164	Street lights
0165	Street signs

0170	**Signage**
0171	Temporary
0172	Permanent

0180	**Landscaping**
0181	Sod or seed
0182	Shrubs
0183	Trees
0184	Mulch
0185	Other materials
0186	Other labor

0190	**Amenities**
0191	Swimming pool
0192	Tennis courts
0193	Tot lots
0194	Putting greens
0195	Exercise trail